The Evidential Details Mystery Series

Decorated United States Military Intelligence Psychic
Remote Viewer solves some of History's Greatest Mysteries

U.S. Legion of Merit Medal

Jack the Ripper

State Secret

Seeds/McMoneagle

©2020

The Logistics News Network, LLC.

Evidential Details

The Quick Take

Mr. McMoneagle was awarded the U.S. Military's Legion of Merit Award.

"Authority to award the Legion of Merit Medal is reserved for general officers and flag officers in pay grade O-9 (e.g. Lieutenant General and Vice Admiral) and above..." wikipedia.org.

The U.S. Army's Legion of Merit Medal Bestowal Requirements

At least two witnesses must submit seven military forms for a proper medal determination. Based on the quality of the information, Military Decorations Officers selected the medal with the following language.

"The award is given for service rendered in a clearly exceptional manner. For service not related to actual war the term **"key individual"** applies to a narrower range of positions than in time of war and requires evidence of **significant achievement**. In peacetime, service should be in the nature of a special requirement or of an **extremely difficult duty** performed in an **unprecedented and clearly exceptional manner."**

Once it was confirmed what this soldier could do, the U.S. Joint Chiefs of Staff and the following agencies requested his services.

"During his career, Mr. McMoneagle has provided ...informational support to the Central Intelligence Agency **(CIA)**, Defense Intelligence Agency **(DIA)**, National Security Agency **(NSA)**, Drug Enforcement Agency **(DEA)**, Secret Service, Federal Bureau of Investigation **(FBI)**, United States Customs **(ICE)**, the National Security Council **(NSC)**, most major commands (**Army, Navy, Air Force Intelligence**) within the Department of Defense **(DOD)**, and hundreds of other individuals, companies, and corporations."

Paragraph from Mr. McMoneagle's CV.

Medals Received

Legion of Merit

Meritorious Service

Citations

Meritorious Service with **one** Oak Leaf Cluster;[1]
Army Commendation with **two** Oak Leaf Clusters, Presidential Unit;
Meritorious Unit with **three** Oak Leaf Clusters;
Vietnam Gallantry Cross with Palm for gathering enemy intelligence in advance of Allied counter offensives.

---

[1] The same medal cannot be given twice. When exemplary service is again rendered, the Oak Leaf Cluster (OLC) is awarded in place of a second identical medal.

JOSEPH W. MCMONEAGLE
Chief Warrant Officer
U. S. Army
330th Radio Reconnaissance Company
Pleiku-An Khe-Tet
Vietnam

Legion of Merit

MEDALS-CITATIONS: Meritorious Service w/1 OLC, Army Commendation w/2 OLC, Presidential Unit, Meritorious Unit w/3 OLC, Vietnam Gallantry Cross w/Palm

Operated in the Central Highlands gathering vital enemy intelligence for counter offensives.

2nd Field Force

The Bronze Plaque
on the Brick Wall

In what is clearly the most fascinating component of U.S. Military History, Joseph McMoneagle is the only man in world history to be awarded a medal for consistent accuracy in Controlled Remote Viewing (Psy-functioning) by a military. As *Operation Star Gate's* Number 1 Military Intelligence asset at Fort Meade, Maryland, he was the Pentagon's go to man when secret data could not be obtained by any other means or was time sensitive.

Conceptual Nomenclature

The worst term of all is "psychic." No stable definition has ever been established for it, and there are great hazards in attempting to utilize a term which has not much in the way of an agreed upon definition.

Supporters do assume that it refers to extraordinary, non-normal (para-normal) activities of mind. But skeptics assume it refers to illusion, derange-ment and a variety of non-normal or abnormal clinical psychopathologies."

Remote Viewing - One of the Superpowers of the Human Bio-Mind; Remote Viewing and its Conceptual Nomenclature Problems by Ingo Swann (09Jan96)

Military Targeting Follow-up

"Det G's[2] viewers looked at projects ranging from the status of a cement plant in a hostile country to the location of Soviet troops in Cuba. Important North Korean personalities were targeted, as well as underground facilities in Europe, chemical weapons in Afghanistan, the presence of electronic bugs in the new U.S. embassy in Moscow, the activities of a KGB general officer, a missing U.S. helicopter, tunnels under the Korean De-militarized Zone, and numerous buildings whose purposes were unknown to U.S. Intelligence."

"But frequently we never learned how close we had come to the truth, how helpful we had been, or even what we had been looking for in the first place. The targets were sometimes so highly classified that substantive evaluations could not be provided."

---

[2] Det G [Detachment G] was the remote viewing program's code name as it evolved from Operation 'Gondola Wish' to Operation 'Grill Flame'. These were the viewers to make the Army's cut between December 1978 and January 1979. "The Army Chief of Staff for Intelligence, Major General Thompson, officially decreed that the program name, embodied in Det G, would be the focal point for all Army involvement in parapsychology and remote viewing." Op cit. Smith

The Evidential Details Mysteries Series

Jack the Ripper – State Secret includes biographical references.

The Evidential Details
Imprint is a Division of the
Logistics News Network, LLC.

RV Session Work ©1997
Publication release ©2019
Updated 2020
All rights reserved

History – British – Nineteenth Century – Crime – Serial Murder - Queen Victoria – Disraeli, Benjamin – Stride, Elizabeth - Unsolved Mysteries – Military Intelligence Controlled Remote Viewing - McMoneagle, Joseph W. – Puthoff PhD., Dr. Harold E. – Stanford Research Institute – Neurophysiology - Anomalous Cognition – Quantum Entanglement

Book design by Logistics News Network, LLC.
ISBN: 9780982692851
Library of Congress Card Number:

Printed in the United States of America

If you are unable to purchase this, or our other history books in your local bookstore, visit our web site at **www.EvidentialDetails.com**

Preface

This is the first English language manuscript to present the life story of Lizbeth Gustafsdotter Ericson Stride as the central personality. But it is not the first published. We determined Jack was Aaron Kosminski in 1997 and sat on the material until 2019 – 22 years. Out of respect we declined to be the first to reveal Jack's ethnicity. We also understood why established "Ripperologists" had not named him even though they likely knew.

In 1999 I requested a friend ask his Rabbi our findings. While I expected condemnation as an anti-Semite, the practical answer came back, "It would depend on how it was written." This served as acknowledgement we got it right. But it also threw the ball back into our court.

What the public does not understand about the Ripper case is that it is actually a two part event.

1) The crimes, investigation and apprehension of the Ripper;
2) The problems of silently subverting capital punishment with life time incarceration without due process.

This book is the first to pursue item two with the release of Russell Edwards' *Naming Jack the Ripper* (Lyon Press, ISBN978-1-4930-3894-7), and the subsequent press coverage partially presented in the Foreword.

In 1997 there was little on the Internet, just scattered pieces written about Stride in the English language. This has changed due to the trail she left. Her Swedish farm girl, to hooker, to disaster victim, to Ripper casualty is engaging and renders this book a woman's story. But then to discover she was involved in interpersonal social conduct so rare it was undocumented in medical literature turned out to be astounding.

Additionally, we introduce military intelligence controlled remote viewing nomenclature by providing the Princess Diana material. This was in preparation for the Maybrick data. For this target we compared James Maybrick's energy signature with the murderer in the Dutfield Yard alley. This is an established exercise within the Star Gate black ops tasking capability.

Chicago – 2020

For murder, though it have no tongue, will speak.

Shakespeare in *Hamlet*

Table of Contents

Foreword

When writing a book series unleashing answers to previously unsolved mysteries, one is tasked with selecting a rounded topics group. In this case it was to add a crime blotter mystery to the series. During the 1990's the greatest of these was Jack the Ripper.

Obviously the answer was unknown until the receipt of the report with drawings. Once brought forward, it can offend ancestral families, governments, the religious, or cultural minorities. This series was never intended to smear anyone. Then in March of 2019, the scientific findings of others made it acceptable to release this material. Below you will find some of the fair use news articles that made this possible.

Science Magazine - March 15, 2019
www.sciencemag.org/news/2019/03/does-new-genetic-analysis-finally-reveal-identity-jack-ripper

Does a new genetic analysis finally reveal the identity of Jack the Ripper? By David Adam

"This isn't the first time Kosminski has been linked to the crimes. But it is the first time the supporting DNA evidence has been published in a peer-reviewed journal. The first genetic tests on shawl samples were conducted several years ago by (Dr.) Jari Louhelainen, a biochemist at Liverpool John Moores University in the United Kingdom…

In what Louhelainen and his colleague David Miller, a reproduction and sperm expert at the University of Leeds in the United Kingdom, claim is "the most systematic and most advanced genetic analysis to date regarding the Jack the Ripper murders," they describe extracting and amplifying the DNA from the shawl. The tests compared fragments of mitochondrial DNA—the portion of DNA inherited only from one's mother—retrieved from the shawl with samples taken from living descendants of Eddowes and Kosminski. The DNA matches that of a living relative of Kosminski, they conclude in the Journal of Forensic Sciences.

Science News - Thursday, 11 September, 2014

"The shawl, owned by businessman Russell Edwards, who bought it at auction in 2007, was tested by Dr. David Miller, of the School of Medicine at the University of Leeds. He said: "I was able to identify body cells that were consistent with the presence of seminal fluid on the shawl and which enabled us to match DNA with the descendants of one of the suspected killers, Polish immigrant Aaron Kosminski.

As well as studying the cells' DNA, the team at Liverpool John Moores University also studied a blood stain that was on the shawl. Seven small segments of mitochondrial DNA, passed down through the direct female line, were isolated from the blood stains and matched with the DNA of Karen Miller, a direct descendant of (victim) Catherine Eddowes. This confirmed the presence of Eddowes' blood on the item of clothing.

In addition to identifying DNA on the shawl, a further investigation was made by experts into the provenance of the shawl. The blue dye on it was tested using nuclear magnetic resonance techniques, which found that the shawl was Russian (Kosminski's) and predates the murders.

Fox News - Mar. 15, 2019

Jack the Ripper revealed? DNA research may finally unravel mystery by James Rogers

"We applied novel, minimally destructive techniques for sample recovery from forensically relevant stains on the evidence and separated single cells linked to the suspect, followed by phenotypic analysis," say the scientists, in the Journal of Forensic Sciences. "The mtDNA [mitochondrial DNA] profiles of both the victim and the suspect matched the corresponding reference samples, fortifying the link of the evidence to the crime scene.

Genomic DNA from single cells recovered from the evidence was amplified, and the phenotypic information acquired matched the only witness statement regarded as reliable," said Louhelainen and Miller, in the(ir) abstract.

Biology - September 8, 2014 - Updated October 20, 2015

DNA testing reportedly reveals identity of Jack the Ripper

A report in the (Daily) Mail on Sunday names the killer as Aaron Kosminski, a Jewish Polish-born immigrant who lived in the East End and would have been 23 years old at the time of the murders.

Molecular biologist Dr. Jari Louhelainen tells the Mail on Sunday that he used a technique called "vacuuming" to remove DNA from a stained shawl purportedly belonging to one of the victims, Catherine Eddowes.

The scientist said that infrared imaging revealed that the stains on the shawl were blood stains and were consistent with arterial blood splatter caused by slashing. (Dr.) Louhelainen claimed that the DNA from the blood stains found on the shawl was a match for Eddowes.

Evidential Details

Other stains found on the shawl were florescent and had the characteristics of semen. Louhelainen said that a second set of DNA tests were carried out on the stains after cells from the epithelium -- a tissue that lines cavities and organs -- were discovered in the stains. Two strands of DNA were tested against a descendent of Kosminski's sister. The first was a 99.2 percent match, while the other strand was a perfect match. Louhelainen wrote that the DNA extracted from the shawl enabled him to specify Eddowes's killer as being of Russian Jewish ancestry with dark hair.

A contemporary artist's depiction of the phantom Jack the Ripper.

Come, thick night,
And pall thee in the dunnest smoke of hell.
That my keen knife see not the wound it makes.

Shakespeare in *Macbeth*

Introduction

To Remote

Viewing

A review of the terminology, history
and capabilities in the targeting of

The Former Princess
Of Wales Diana Spencer's
1997 Auto Accident

(For the cover story, please refer to the Table of Contents)

"When they (University researchers) did produce an incredibly accurate response during an experiment, it was in even a moderate sense "unnerving." In a greater sense, it was "earth shattering." As (Stanford PhD) Russell (Targ) implied, for some it was even "terrifying". In no case, was it ever taken lightly, as it always had a tendency to alter one's perspective towards reality and/or our place within it."

~ Medal Recipient Joseph W. McMoneagle~

Evidential Details

It was the peak of the Twentieth Century's Cold War [1945-1990]. The United States, the old Soviet Union, and the People's Republic of China were striving to find new ways to get an intelligence edge. During the years 1968 to 1972, the United States obtained reports that scientists in the Soviet Union had had some success with a telekinesis program that introduced atrial fibulation into frog hearts causing a heart attack. Realizing the program could target key military and political leaders, and so driven by a threat assessment, the Central Intelligence Agency funded a Stanford University think tank in Menlo Park, California - the Stanford Research Institute (SRI) - to conduct an analysis about what humanity through the ages has pondered. The doctors were to determine scientifically if psy-functioning could be taught, quantified and directed within written protocols. If so, did this represent a credible threat to the people of the United States? Their highly classified "Black Ops" program lasted from early 1972 until November 1995.

Under the most extensive and stringent experimentation that two PhD's could devise, the SRI, supported by other labs and the Army, developed mankind's first "psychic" protocols. "This led to greater under-standing of everything from methods of evaluation, to establishing statistical standards, to how a human brain might be appropriately studied."[i] When their findings were made public, many in the academic community were privately stunned.

Eventually this covert military effort focused on real world data collection. As the years of research, analysis and application moved through the 1970's and 80's, Army brass with wholly personal motives, would attempt to quash the program even when research costs did not impact their budget. "All the funding had been approved on a year-to-year basis, and only then based on how effective the unit was in supporting the tasking agencies. These reviews were made semi-annually at the Senate and House select subcommittee level, where the work results were reviewed within the context in which it was happening."[ii]

Fortunately, for The People, the program was given different code names and moved around various Defense budgets until much of the research and development was completed. What emerged was an incredibly "robust" database - and a process - referred to as Controlled Remote Viewing [CRV].[1] [This may also stand for Coordinate Remote Viewing when longitudinal and latitudinal target coordinates are used.]

Much of the work took place within the 902nd United States Army Intelligence Group at Fort Meade, Maryland, whose barracks have been demolished. However, from the fastidiously maintained database emerged statistically advanced practitioners; world class viewers whose RV data was the "best in the business." Among these, one remote viewer was the first in history to be decorated with the Army's Legion of Merit and Meritorious Service Awards (with five Oak Leaf Clusters) for having made key contributions to the Intelligence community. This same individual was tasked to unlock the mysteries in this Evidential Details Book Series.

Obviously, accuracy is the name of the game. As with any horizon application process, purposefully moving the human brain into what is entanglement at the sub-quark level required new clinical terminology. As the CRV process was tested, protocols written and cautiously modified, scientists documented mental hazards to viewer accuracy. These hind-rances were cataloged and their characteristics differentiated. Year after year laboratory research determined accurate mental representations could be inhibited in a variety of ways. Some of these mental distracters included:

Physical Inclemency - Knowledge of an expected disruption like a phone call or someone about to arrive during a remote viewing session.

Advanced Visuals - A thought you cannot get rid of before a session.

Emotional Distracters or Attractors - An image you do or do not want to view regardless of the tasking.

Front Loading - Knowledge of what the target is before the viewing session. If localized, it can be used in targeting a feature within the whole picture, perhaps a house in a meadow in front of a mountain. However, without neutral wording like "The target is man-made" the object is generally rendered unworkable.

Analytic Overlay [AOL] - If a viewer is not informed about the target and not front loaded but still has personal information about it, that knowledge may pollute the information stream rendering the session unworkable. Analytic Overlay can be a problem for any viewer. According to the military's former #1 remote viewer:

Joseph McMoneagle - Analytic overlay - CRV [Controlled Remote Viewing], **as a format or method for learning remote viewing, offers a structure within which you can discard or identify specific elements within a session for which you are certain or not certain. Analytic Over-Lay (AOL) being a common label for something that falls within the "uncertain" category. However, when studied (under laboratory con-ditions), there is evidence that fifty percent of the time, information labeled as AOL actuality, wasn't.**

I have observed just as many times, someone being smacked up against the side of the head while attempting CRV because they had strayed from the given format and slipped into AOL. I think that sometimes you may forget that CRV was developed within the hallowed halls of SRI and was taught there for years. I saw very little

difference in the AOL pitfalls with CRV and other methodologies. I did see that to some extent it was a highly polished technique, which was more easily transferred through training.

With this quick review of the subconscious transference of recollections, we turn to the remote viewing of the Princess Diana Spencer's accident in the early morning hours of August 31, 1997. As this researcher found, how one targets is critical to the result. In the fall of 1997, the massive press coverage of Princess Diana's accident and funeral emerged as a very real overlay problem. The Hotel Ritz in Paris, France rather than the crash site was targeted. There had been much less news coverage at the hotel. At the time, this target was less than two months old. No accident report had been completed. An envelope, with a second target envelope inside, had been mailed to Joseph McMoneagle's home with nothing more than the targeting coordinates and a date. A skeptical *Life Magazine* reporter was on hand as an observer to write a story.

Mr. McMoneagle requested I submit a target. The viewing event started at 11:49 am on October 29, 1997. What makes these sessions interesting is that the reader can sense the Intelligence intellect. Having viewed 1200 targets in just the last two years of the military's Operation Star Gate alone, this job would reasonably have been assigned to the only viewer to participate in the program for twenty-three years. What was submitted was:

Target Envelope No. 102997 - (no additional information other than what's sealed within the envelope.)

* * *

As her size nine shoes hit the airport tarmac the former Princess of Wales Diana Spencer, 36, knew she was entitled to an escort by that special branch of the French Interior Ministry charged with guarding visiting dignitaries - the Service de Protection des Hautes Personalities (SPHP). But there would be no need of the service once she left the airport. This was to be a private visit.

Diana was returning from a yachting vacation in the Mediterranean off Northeast Sardinia. She and Emad "Dodi" Al-Fayed, [1955-1997] had been aboard the Fayed family's $27 million dollar (US$39.5m/2015), 195 foot yacht *Jonikal,* with 16 crew members.

At this point, "...in her relationship with Dodi Fayed she was displaying a new facet. In some ways a late developer, she had grown up and was simply having some adult fun."[iii] But the couple had been stalked by highfspeed paparazzi boats wherever they went. On their last afternoon, they came ashore at the Cala de Volpe in Sardinia and the, "Paparazzi swarmed around them like bees, flashing away."[iv] Forced back to the boat, "Things came to a head when a scuffle broke out between three paparazzi and several members of the *Jonikal*'s crew."[v]

At about the same time, hundreds of miles away, a 73 year-old grandfather, Edward Williams, walked into the police station in Mountain Ash, Mid Glamorgan, Wales. He reported to the police he had had a premonition Princess Diana was going to die. The police log, time stamped 14:12 hours on August 27, 1997, stated:

"He [Williams] *said he was a psychic and predicted that Princess Diana was going to die. In previous years he has predicted that the Pope and Ronald Reagan were going to be the victims of assassination. On both occasions he was proven to be correct. Mr. Williams appeared to be quite normal."*[vi]

Based on his previous record the police passed this report along to the department's Special Branch Investigative Unit.

Fed up with the non-stop press hassle, on Saturday August 30, Dodi and Diana boarded the Fayed's Gulfstream IV jet at Olbia airport in Sardinia and flew north. They arrived at Le Bourget Airport about 10 miles north of Paris, France at 3:20 p.m. Fayed's butler Rene Delorm recalled, "Unfortunately, we had a welcoming committee of about ten paparazzi waiting for us."[vii] About 600 feet (183 meters) away was a Mercedes and a Range Rover. "We had all seen the paparazzi, so we moved quickly. We wanted to get out of the plane and into the cars as fast as possible. (Body Guard) Trevor (Rees-Jones) was the first out of the jet..."[viii]

The entourage had a police escort from the airport up to France's highway A-1 leading to Paris. But as they entered the expressway, reporter's cars and two man motorcycle teams immediately dogged the entourage. The paparazzi were armed with powerful, maximum strength, flashes to penetrate deep into the car. Philippe Dourneau, 35, was Dodi's chauffeur. But in the Range Rover vehicle there had been a switch. At the wheel was the Assistant Chief of Hotel Security Henri Paul. It is unclear why Paul was chauffeuring that afternoon and not at the Ritz Hotel as acting Security Chief.

Once on the highway, Dodi instructed Ritz Hotel driver Dourneau to pick up speed in an attempt to elude photographers. What ensued was a high speed pursuit with motorcycle cameramen weaving in and out shooting pictures. The motorcycle whirl was so intense Diana reportedly cried out in alarm that someone could get killed.[ix]

The photographer's strategy was to slow the convoy down. "Then a black car sped ahead of us and ducked in front of the Mercedes, braking and making us slow down so the paparazzi on motorcycles could get more pictures. They were risking their lives and ours, just to get a shot of Dodi and Diana riding in a car. "*Unbelievable*", exclaimed butler Rene Delorm.[x]

Dodi was not accustomed to this and after their high seas harassment, his patience was running thin. Pursuing for miles, the paparazzi then used phones to notify photographers ahead to form another gauntlet on the next highway segment. The Fayed cars split up in an attempt to divide the photographers. Some pursued Henri Paul as he drove to Dodi's apartment to deliver the luggage.

Finally, the Mercedes made it to Bois de Boulogne on the outskirts of Paris to visit the Fayed's Windsor Villa. They arrived about 3:45 p.m. Then they were off to the Ritz Hotel in downtown Paris at 4:35. Alerted by the cameramen the hotel entrance was by now packed with photographers which in turn generated curiosity seekers in the general public.

Once inside the hotel, Diana checked into the second floor Imperial Suite and went to have her hair done. She also made some phone calls. After the accident, London's *Daily Mail* correspondent Richard Kay stated that Diana had called him saying she was going to complete her contractual obligations through November and then go into private life.

Another call was made to psychic Rita Rogers whom Diana had been in contact with since 1994. Three weeks earlier, on August 12, Dodi and Di had visited Rogers for a reading on Dodi. She warned him not to go driving in Paris. "*I saw a tunnel, motorcycles, there was this tremendous sense of speed.*"[xi] Uneasy, Rogers reminded Diana about her readout concerning a Parisian tunnel saying, "...*remember what I told Dodi.*"[xii]

At seven o'clock, they left the hotel for Dodi's apartment at Rue 1 Arsene-Houssaye arriving at 7:15 p.m. Here the couple found the street so crowded they could not even open the car door. "The paparazzi literally mobbed the couple," said (32 year old former Royal Marine Kes) Wingfield. "They really disturbed and frightened the Princess, even though she was used to this. These paparazzi were shouting, which made them even more frightening. I had to push them back physically.'"[xiii]

From their third floor apartment, butler Rene recalled:

"...*I could see they were being mobbed. I heard the shouting, saw the flashes going off and watched a security guard shove one of the photographers. Dodi did his best to shield Diana as Trevor and Kes fought to clear a path to the door... The princess was ashen and trembling, and Dodi was angry as they stalked through the apartment door...*"[xiv]

This was the way it was going to be. Rumors were rife about a marriage proposal and some wealthy publishers made it clear big money was available to the photographer that got the "million dollar shot". But no million dollars had been budgeted.

Later, after things settled down and Dodi had returned from shopping for two rings at the Repossi Jewelry Boutique, Rene recounted, "I met Dodi as he walked through the kitchen doorway, his eyes gleaming with excitement. It was then that he showed me the ring. *'Make sure we have champagne on ice when we come back from dinner,'* he told me urgently. *'I'm going to propose to her tonight!'"*[xv] Elated, he also phoned this proposal news to his cousin Hassan Yassin that evening.[xvi] [Dodi received a US\$100,000/month (\$146.5/2015) allowance from his father.]

Dodi had the Hotel staff book a 9:45 p.m. dinner reservation at the fashionable restaurant Chez Benoit on the Rue Saint Martin. He also phoned the Ritz staff he would not be returning. As a result, Security Chief Henri Paul departed for the weekend at 7:05 p.m.

At 9:30 p.m., Dodi and Diana left the apartment for dinner but could not get through the crowd at the restaurant entrance. It was clear they could not enter a restaurant together. The enormous number of paparazzi forced Dodi to cancel their night out. The Press was controlling his special night with his special lady. A frustrated Dodi decided they should make the four mile drive to the Hotel Ritz where they could dine in France's only "safe" restaurant. But Security Chief Henri Paul had gone for the weekend and the abrupt change in plans left the hotel staff with no time to prepare for their arrival.

When they arrived at the Ritz, another press riot broke out. It took Diana two whole minutes to negotiate the camera gauntlet the 20 feet from the front door drive-up to the hotel turnstile. The security camera time stamped her entrance at 9:53 p.m. Security man Wingfield said: *"I had to protect her physically from the paparazzi, who were coming really too close to her. Their cameras were right next to her face."*[xvii]

Dodi was now furious and started shouting at his employees about no security to shield the 10 second walk up from the driveway. Shaken, the press savvy Diana wept in the lobby. Everyone was upset. With the owner's son angry, and the security force completely embattled, a decision was made to call the Security Chief back to work. Francois Tendil called Henri Paul's cell phone at 9:55 p.m.

Once safely in their room, Dodi called his father Mohammed Al-Fayed at approximately 10:00 p.m. He said the two would announce their engagement the next week when Diana returned from England.[xviii] "Diana always had the children for the last few days before they went back to school at the start of a new term, so that she could get everything ready and make sure they had the right kit."[xix] On Friday, she had called to confirm her boys would be at the airport to meet her on Sunday morning.

Dinner was ordered from the hotel's Imperial Suite restaurant.

Diana's last meal was scrambled eggs with mushrooms and asparagus, then vegetable tempura with fillet of sole. As Di and Dodi were trying to dine normally, Henri Paul pushed his way back into the hotel.

For this targeting, the Hotel Ritz Building was tasked using the proper date, time, and location coordinates. As Mr. McMoneagle looked at a double blind envelope on his dining room table, he started:

McMoneagle - I find myself standing next to a man who is inside some kind of a public building. He is approximately five feet, ten inches in height, good build, good condition physically. He weighs about 165 pounds, is clean shaven, light brown hair, right handed, 38-40 years of age, and is not British or American; meaning he probably has another language other than English as his native tongue.[3]

Upon his return, Henri Paul waited around the Ritz for about two hours. He allegedly had a couple drinks at the bar. The Ritz security cameras recorded his behavior which would be used for future analysis. As Chief of Security, he was certainly aware of their placement and recording capabilities.

McMoneagle - Building interior - Where he (Paul) is within the building is inside of a very elaborate corridor. It runs the full length of the building and has lots of gilded paint, mirrors, thick carpets, lots of flowers, and is very fancy. The corridor runs straight out to a front entry which is well lit and very busy (even though my sense is that it is very late at night). There is an area off to the right of this corridor which has a lot of dark paneling and dark colors with a long bar or type of counter. So, this may be the reception area of the hotel or something like that.

Where he (Paul) is standing is where the main corridor intersects with a short corridor that runs off at a ninety degree angle to the left. It intersects with some kind of a smaller staff or receiving area; perhaps a back door to the building. It is recessed and that is where his car is parked.

The Etoile Limousine Company manager Jean-Francis Musa, 39, provided six cars to the Ritz Hotel for their exclusive use. This Mercedes was licensed as a Grande Remise auto meaning only a licensed chauffeur was authorized to drive it. Henri Paul did not possess those credentials.

McMoneagle - Driver orientation - I believe that he (Paul) drives a cab or limo...on the side, because I associate him with a car, which is parked outside and he is thinking about this car, or it seems to occupy his thoughts for some reason. He is mostly interested with driving from

---

[3] Paul was 167 lbs. and he was 41 years old. He had brown hair and was also balding. His native language was French. He spoke fluent English and some German.

point A to point B. I believe he is not alone and get a strong feeling of mixed male/female in energy; which either means his passenger will be gay, or consist of two people--a male and a female.

Limo is not a stretch limo but a short, black and formal kind of car. I get an impression of a Mercedes emblem or some kind of emblem like that, so I'm assuming it is a very expensive car, could be a Mercedes. It is formal and black with an extended foot space in the back seat. Four doors. It is very heavy and my sense is that it might be equipped for important passengers — e.g., bullet proof glass, armoring, hardened tires, etc.; which leads me to believe that at least one of the passengers [Trevor Rees-Jones, 29] **might be a bodyguard** [but] **this may be Analytic overlay caused by the excessive feelings of security surrounding this vehicle and driver.** [4]

* * *

Information about Henri Paul's mixed motivations have come to light in the years since the accident. Born one of five brothers on July 3, 1956 in the port town of Lorient, France, he had a Bachelors Degree in Mathematics and Science from the Lycee St. Louis and had won several contests for his skill as a classical pianist. He became a pilot in 1976 but was unable to qualify as a jet fighter pilot when he joined the French Air

In 1986, Paul helped setup Ritz Security. He went on to become Assistant Director. On the day of the accident, he was carrying 12,560 francs (US $2,280) and his savings account passbook. Where the money came from is unknown, but he was one of only two men in France that had access to the automobile conversations of Dodi and Di. The ability to advise the press of their plans would have been of great value. [Henri Paul may have charged the equivalent of US$2,250 (1997) per surveillance event and simply had an additional $30 pocket money that day. His salary was reported at $40,000 ($58,600/2015) per year.]

Personal adversity. Henry Paul had recently been passed over for promotion a second time by Hotel Ritz management. The first disappointment had come on Jan 1, 1993 when the nod went to colleague Jean Hocquet even though Paul was obviously in position as the number two security man. Now again, effective June 30, 1997, as Deputy Chief, he be-

---

[4] The Mercedes S 280 sedan, valued at about $100,000 (US$146.520/2015) was engineered with eight advanced safety systems. The car had a reinforced chassis and roof. It had energy absorbing front and rear end crumple zones with electronic traction control. It also had an electronic ESP sensing system, which monitored trajectory with wheel speed to sense cornering speeds.

Session Sketch

This drawing provides a rare glimpse intelligence level RV artwork. In this exercise, people and not the building were targeted. But this sketch could be the third floor at the North Korean Embassy in Moscow, Russia or any building, anywhere, anytime. As a person was the target, the Hotel Ritz Paris first floor was roughed out at midnight on August 31, 1997. Points of interest are:

1) At the top of the page, the words **Big Bldg** appear;
2) The various circles with an **X** inside indicates where people were standing at approximately 12:15 a.m. on August 31, 1997.
3) On the left, the **Main Door** is shown with an **X** representing the doorman. As the hall extends to the right, the various rooms are notated.
4) Toward the bottom is a **Business** area. As you walk from the front door, **"There is an area off to the right of this corridor which has a lot of dark paneling and dark colors with a long bar or type of counter."**
5) At the top is an **Alcove** with two people inside. These individual's backgrounds – conversations – futures – mental states - deaths can be targeted at any time in the future.
6) Where the hallway comes to a junction there is a **Man**. This is Henri Paul as he monitors the activities in both corridors. What were Paul's private thoughts? **"I associate him with a car which is parked outside and he is thinking about this car, or it seems to occupy his thoughts for some reason."**
7) Behind Henri Paul is the **Laborer Area**. Next to this is the drawing date and time documenting who was where when.
8) The hallway to the **Side Door**, **"...intersects with some kind of a smaller staff or receiving area; perhaps a back door to the building. It is recessed and that is where his car is parked."** That recessed area is shown.
9) McMoneagle also shows the **Formal Black Limo**'s position by the back door and correctly identified the automobile's color and manufacturer's hood ornament. (bottom right)

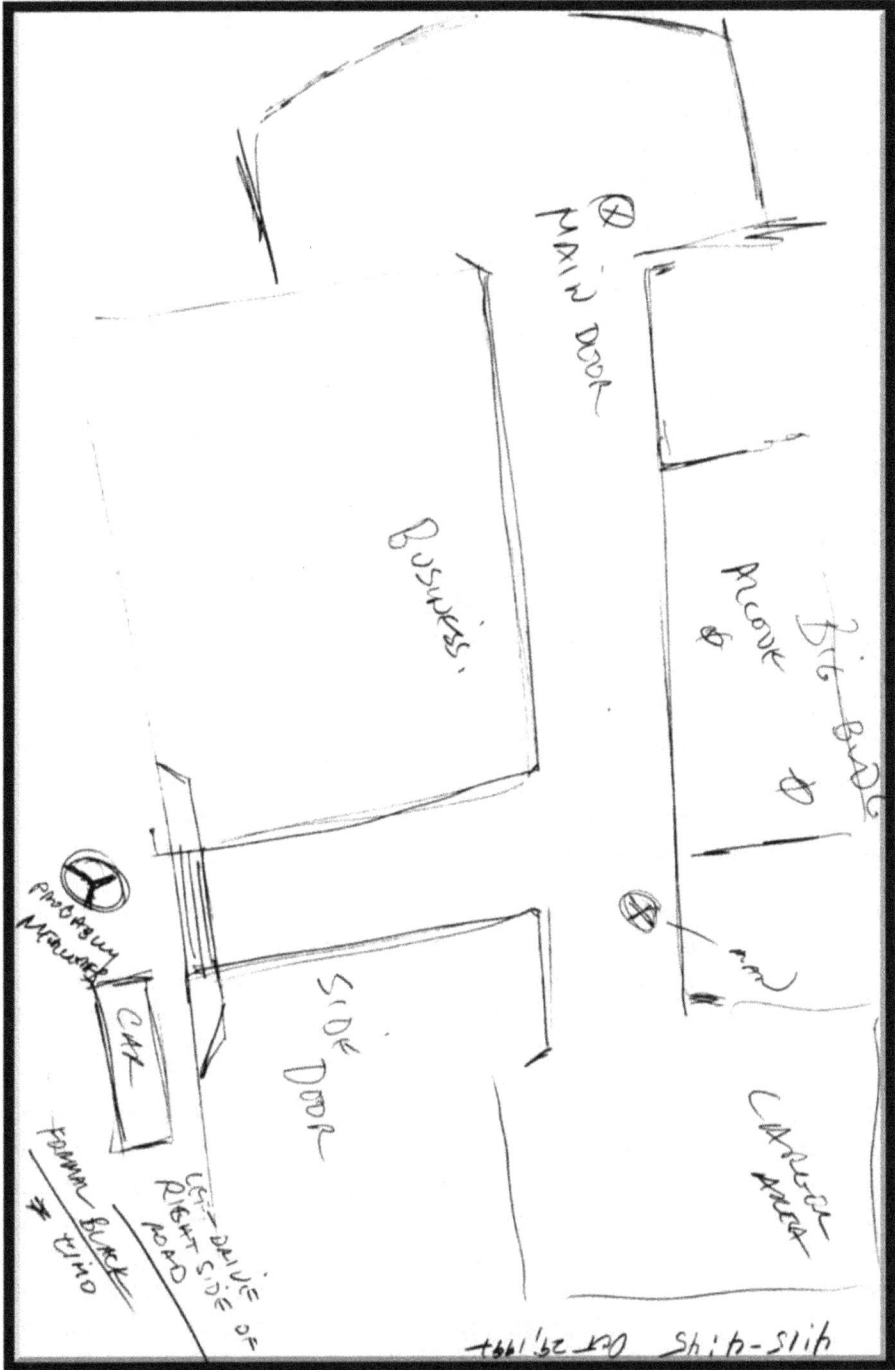

Hotel Ritz Paris first floor with Mercedes (lower right) as viewed from Virginia, USA.

came the defacto head of a twenty person security team while Ritz Management searched for another chief. Now vulnerable, Paul had been informed of this exactly one month before the accident.

Post mortem tests stated Paul had consumed two antidepressants called Fluoxetine and Tiapride before the accident. Fluoxetine is the active ingredient in Prozac and together these drugs are commonly used to fight alcoholism. When alcohol is introduced, the intoxicant effect is multiplied. On September 17, a more sophisticated laboratory's final report was issued. It stated that Henri Paul had been in, *"moderate chronic alcoholism for a minimum of one week."*[xx] Once this became public, the Ritz's attorneys and Mohammed Al-Fayed found themselves on the defensive. An unlicensed employee now appeared criminally negligent in a multiple wrongful death accident while in Hotel Ritz employment. It became the million dollar picture vs. the Al-Fayeds

The intoxication driving limit in France is 0.50 grams per liter. One lab report stated Henri Paul's blood alcohol level was 1.87 g/l. This is the equivalent drinking time for eight or nine shots of whiskey in what was found to be an empty stomach. A second, private laboratory's more moderate findings were used in the Final Report. The Paris Prosecutor's Office Report stated:

"On this particular point, numerous expert's reports examined following the autopsy on the body of Henri Paul rapidly showed the presence of a level of pure alcohol per litre of blood of between 1.73 and 1.75 grams, which is far superior, in all cases, than the legal level.

Similarly, these analyses revealed as [did] those carried out on samples of the hair and bone marrow of the deceased, that he regularly consumed Prozac and Tiapridal, both medicines which are not recommended for drivers, as they provoke a change in the ability to be vigilant, particularly when they are taken in combination with alcohol."[xxi]

So had Henri Paul been out drinking? It is known he returned to the Ritz two hours and fifty minutes after departing. But no one knew where he was or what he was doing when he received the Ritz phone call. Subsequent investigations about who had seen Paul during this period failed to provide a single witness. In Paris, in the fall of 1997, there was a real fear of liability for anyone acknowledging Paul had been drinking in their establishment. Nonetheless, the French press reported *"someone"* saw Paul drinking "aperitifs" between 7:05 and 10:08 p.m. that evening. "Someone" is wide open. It means that after he got the call to return at 9:55 p.m., he dallied almost another quarter-hour before departing which is hard to believe given

Dodi's concerns. Until now, the critical question about where and what Paul was doing before returning to the hotel remained unknown.

McMoneagle - I think he was in fact sitting in a small restaurant or coffee shop, very near where he lives. Maybe even on the corner near his house. He was alone as far as I can tell. I think he was in fact drinking coffee. I do not think he was depressed, at least not more than usual. Also, regardless of what might be said, I <u>DID NOT</u> get a sense that he was drunk. It is remotely possible that he was taking some kind of a medication but I doubt it.

Coffee! Not drunk! This flew in the face of the formal investigation. We were now privately aware, months before the controversy started, Henri Paul was not drunk.

Henri Paul was a pilot. Research indicated it was impossible to reconcile allegations of alcoholism with Paul's recent physical examination. Unbeknownst to the authorities, just two days before the accident, Paul had completed a "rigorous" physical examination to renew his pilot's license. His *Certificat D'Aptitude Physique et Mentale* showed, "No signs of alcoholism."[xxii] A direct medical conflict supporting McMoneagle. Was Paul really fighting alcoholism? Six months after these sessions, the Ritz Hotel security videos further reaffirmed our data.

Behavioral Psychologist Dr. Martin Skinner commented in Fulcrum Productions documentary for ITV. The doctor stated there were no behavioral signs of drunkenness as Henri Paul waited for Dodi and Diana.

Skinner: *I don't think there is evidence, from the video, that can suggest he looked drunk. The pictures of him walking up and down the corridor are straight and smooth. He is standing very still and there is nothing in his demeanor, from these videos, to suggest that there are any problems with his competence in this situation.*[xxiii]

Next came a statement from Trevor Rees-Jones, the front seat bodyguard sitting next to Paul. About intoxication, he said:

Rees-Jones: *I had no reason to suspect he was drunk. He did not look or sound like he had been drinking. He just seemed his normal self. He was working. He was competent. End of story. I can state quite categorically that he was not a hopeless drunk as some have tried to suggest. I like to think I have enough intelligence to see if the guy was plastered or not – and he wasn't.*[xxiv]

Neither the bodyguards, nor Dodi, or anyone else at the Hotel detected anything unusual in Paul's behavior. But there was more.

Paul's blood was next reported as containing abnormally high carbon monoxide levels - twenty percent too much. How this happened has never been determined. But doctors agree it is impossible for a forty year old man, with that much poison in his blood stream, not to look and feel sick - too sick for high speed urban driving. When the press advanced the idea car exhaust was the source of Paul's poisoning, Dodi's father, Mohammed Al-Fayed, put the obvious question: *"How did Henri Paul get 20% carbon monoxide in his blood when my son had none?"*[xxv]

The obvious question is how you can get that much CO^2 into someone's blood stream when, due to an instantaneous death there was no breathing, and the engine had stopped.

During his last month Henri Paul had come to know what it was like to assume the Security Chief's responsibilities while the Ritz Hotel interviewed. He must have been concerned an outside hire may not be as accommodating as his previous colleague boss had been. After setting up the Ritz security operation, and with a decade of service, Henri Paul now faced the possibility of being forced out by a new supervisor uneasy about his hotel security experience. Clearly, Ritz management was not taking care of Paul as a career professional. [5]

Another component of the Henri Paul enigma concerned the fact that most nations have an Embassy in Paris and many dignitaries and diplomats stay at the Ritz. Stories started to appear that Paul was in the employ of various "foreign and domestic" intelligence services. Then it was discovered he had one million francs [US$200,000–$250,000] spread between eighteen bank accounts in an attempt to disguise the fact. Al-Fayed would later make the claim Paul had spent at least three years working for British intelligence. Where he got this information, or if it is true, is unknown. Paul was also allegedly in contact with the Direction General de la Securite Exterieure [DGSE] - French Intelligence. So, we were left with a feigned alcoholic dead man; with employment and big money surveillance concerns; ordered to violate multiple traffic laws; by a romantically aggravated boss in love with the world's foremost beauty.

Henri Paul was uncertain about his future. He had to have been anxious about protecting his access to the Hotel Ritz time and date stamped video monitoring system. He must have been concerned about his ability to generate good income by documenting high profile business people or foreign dignitary's arrivals and departures.

But all of a sudden, that night there was a positive side to the whole discordant affair. A rare opportunity to make a positive impression on the owner's son was at hand. In the wee hours of August 31, 1997, it would have

[5] The Hotel Ritz subsequently hired a former Scotland Yard Chief Superintendent John MacNamara. His background in criminal intelligence management and investigations was substantially different than Paul's Air Force Reserve security credentials.

been impossible for any driver to presume to caution a provoked Dodi Al-Fayed about safe driving on nearly deserted streets. As characterized by French Union Official Claude Luc:

> *"If one of the Fayeds gives you an order,*
> *you follow it. No questions asked."*[xxvi]

Whatever his prospects, Security Chief Henri Paul was illegally behind the wheel again. He was laid to rest in Lorient, France on September 20, 1997. Father Léon Théraud gave the sermon at Sainte Therese Church.

* * *

On Saturday night, now Sunday morning August 31, a physically aggressive horde of stalkarazzi and other onlookers, estimated at approximately 130 people, jockeyed for position at the front door of the Hotel Ritz Paris. Diana Frances Spencer and her boyfriend Dodi, son of Egyptian born multi-millionaire Mohammad Al-Fayed, needed a second car to exit the hotel's back entrance. Because of the paparazzi, a front door - back door scheme had been set-up for the return to Dodi's apartment. Dodi would take Diana out the back leaving his personal Range Rover in front as a decoy.

McMoneagle – Car is parked on the right side of the road (right side driving) which would rule out England, Bahamas, Hong Kong, Japan, etc. It is night and it is dark. The time for this event is current, probably 1985 to 1997. I will try and bring that down to a shorter period later.

The tag on the limo is elongated, with letters and numbers--which is a European style of tag (License 688 LTV 75). **My sense is that there may actually be two colors of tags on this car, or that it has inter-changeable tags, which are changed, dependent upon where it is being operated. One is yellow with black lettering; the other is white with black lettering. It may be that there are two different colored tags on the car simultaneously—one color on one end, one color on the other.**

This is a superb surveillance example. The yellow license with black lettering was on the rear bumper. As it turned out, the color license designated a private car. The white tag is a "for hire" vehicle. [6] From this the reader can gather the type of information available through remote viewing should this car have been driving a foreign dignitary.

---

[6] In Foreign Relations, these plates could indicate a restricted territory vehicle. If unauthorized, remote viewers could be tasked on who issued both types of plates to the same party. This inquiry would remain secret, while perhaps unmasking a corrupt government official, or a mole in the host country's bureaucracy.

Evidential Details

After some hallway discussion, Ritz chauffeur's Philippe Dourneau and Jean-Francois Musa drove two decoy vehicles to the hotel's front door. The night was clear. The temperature was 77 degrees [25C]. Their engines were revved up as Dodi and Diana hurried out the back door at 12:20 a.m.

A back door security camera photograph time stamped 12:19 a.m. just before they departed. It shows Henri Paul (left) conversing with Dodi and Diana with Trevor Rees-Jones in the background

Diana's last few minutes on earth were now inexorably caught-up in the emotional web of her incensed boyfriend and his driver's employment needs. Some paparazzi across the Rue Cabman observed them as Trevor, Diana, and then Dodi came through the turnstile and got into the Mercedes. Henri Paul pulled out and the chase was on.

McMoneagle - Believe the car is the main focus of this target. The man [Paul] may also be of interest.... I believe this target has to do with an accident that probably occurred either in the very late night hours or possibly very early morning hours. Traffic is very light and the streets are very quiet. Get a sense that there are few cars about, in a place which is usually crawling with cars.

The Mercedes is moving very fast from what apparently is a northwest...direction. Have a sense that it goes over an overpass or cloverleaf kind of interchange which then drops straight down into a tunnel.

The car traveled toward the Seine River's westbound express street referred to as the Cours la Reine. Then they entered the Alexander III & Invalides Tunnel Bridge. The tunnel is 330 meters (361 yards) long.

McMoneagle - It [Mercedes] **then exits the tunnel and covers a large curve of open road which enters another tunnel like area, only this second tunnel is not enclosed completely. Have a sense of concrete tiers on one side... Vehicle is moving very quickly, perhaps in the neighborhood of approximately 100 MPH** [162 km/h], **maybe even a bit faster (in some spurts or straight-aways).**[7]

In my opinion, the driver was driving way beyond the speeds that would have been comfortable for the place and time. I believe he was well trained as a driver but not for the place or speed at which he was driving. I have a sense the driver was doing his damnedest to carry out the instructions of those he was carrying, but was operating at speeds and conditions that even he was never really trained to drive within. I think he was the professional here and was being egged on by the passengers.[8]

A view of their route along the Seine River. The arrow
(top right corner) points the direct route to Fayed's apartment.

These sessions took place approximately ninety days before the release of the official fifty-two page report entitled, *Accident de Passage Souterrain de l'Alma. Paris Dimanche 31 Aout 1997, 0h25. Propostition d'Analyse Scientific et Technique. Synthese et Conclusions.* French Engineer Jean Pietri had been commissioned to write an engineering crash analysis, which went on to verify this earlier remote viewing material.

The distance from the first tunnel to the Pont de l'Alma tunnel is 1.2 kilometers (.75 mile). The speed limit is 30 mph (48km). It is here that

---

[7] The curve in the road is 480 meters [.3 miles] in front of the next tunnel, which provides an acceleration area. But with a subsequent curve and dip, it was not possible to negotiate that section of highway at high speed.

[8] McMoneagle was correct on this detail. Paul had attended special driving courses in Stuttgart, Germany from 1988 through 1993, receiving high marks, and Dodi knew this.

published accounts differ. Apparently, three people witnessed four to six paparazzi motorcycles attempting to pull alongside the speeding Mercedes. Other accounts say the paparazzi were a quarter of a mile behind when the Mercedes entered the tunnel. In either event, it was all futile. Notified by telephone, reporters had already assembled at Dodi's apartment entrance, million dollar picture in mind.

McMoneagle – The Mercedes pulls out to pass a slower moving vehicle at a point in the road where the road ahead rises upward to a secondary overpass. Because of the rise in the road, the driver can't see on-coming traffic in time to avoid it, specifically at this speed.

The final report showed this was correct. French accident investigator Jean Pietri subsequently stated:

"To our surprise, we observed that the field of view is extremely limited. Passing cars disappear from sight well before they actually enter the tunnel because the descending road is obscured by a retaining wall. To the left the field of vision is blocked by a row of trees."[xxvii]

About 40 meters (44 yards) in front of the tunnel the Mercedes hit a gap in the pavement, which further destabilized control. As the car passed a white Fiat Uno at break neck speed Henri Paul saw another car dead ahead.

McMoneagle – I believe he sees an on-coming car which appears to be some kind of a black or dark green sedan. I want to say Citreon, but I'm really not sure. Probably a smaller two door car, two passengers; get a sense of dark green or green-black combination, which could mean a green car (body) **and black** (trim).[9]

Mohammad Medjahdi was driving a Citroen BX with his girlfriend Souad in the tunnel ahead of the Fiat Uno.

McMoneagle – Dodi's last words - Have a fleeting sense that he [Paul] **is being ordered to go faster and to do more erratic things, to avoid something. He is essentially being ordered to do what he is doing.**

To avoid the on-coming traffic, the Mercedes driver swerves hard to the right and catches the small car he is passing [Fiat Uno] **with his rear bumper. Car that was passed was hit. As a result, the Mercedes slews around left, just misses the on-coming car, which** [it] **has just passed, and the driver then begins to over-correct his steering.**

Months after these sessions, French engineers confirmed the Mercedes did nick the Fiat Uno and over corrected to the right. Some tail

---

[9] McMoneagle was obviously in the car looking through the Mercedes windshield. The use of "oncoming" describes the overtaking of cars. It does not refer to opposite direction traffic flow.

light/head light debris was found. Engineers estimated that if the Mercedes was going 100 miles per hour the debris would have rolled sixteen meters (52.5 feet). That hit took place outside the tunnel and it is here the 18.9m (62ft) tire skid mark begins.[10]

McMoneagle - The Mercedes hits the side to left slews across and hits the right, then swings back to the left, where it catches what appears to be a concrete tier or pier (#13 pillar) **of some kind, concrete pilasters, or some kind of upright** (steel reinforced) **concrete dividers, which it hits nearly head on.**

At 12:24 a.m., there was an explosion sound in the tunnel. The subsequent engineering report confirmed Henri Paul's last evasive actions was viewed correctly. Various eyewitnesses recounted the collision. "Gaelle L., 40, a production assistant stated:

"At that moment, in the opposite lane, we saw a large car approaching at high speed. This car swerved to the left, then went back to the right and crashed into the wall with its horn blaring. I should note that in front of this car, there was another, smaller car."[xxviii]

McMoneagle - The Mercedes apparently nearly goes end over end rear to front, but doesn't quite make it [over the top], **instead spinning twice and winds up pointing back in the direction it was coming from.**

The car spinning 1 1/2 times remains unconfirmed. But there was enough inertia for the car to have spun 540 degrees when the rear wheels were off the ground. The impact was so hard that the forward roof area was crushed down to the level of the driver's knees. This is further substantiated by the fact Diana was found facing backward in the back seat, which would not have happened with a simple 180-degree turn. Newsweek Magazine reported French police estimated the car had slowed down to 85 mph at the point of impact.[xxix]

The entire trip had taken about four minutes. Trevor Rees-Jones could only recall the Fiat Uno.

Rees-Jones: *"It seems to me there was one white car with a boot which opened at the back* [hatch back], *and three doors but I don't remember anything else."*[xxx]

He did not leave the hospital until October 4 - thirty-four days later. Aware Henri Paul did not have alcohol in his system we sought clarification

---

[10] The tail light pieces found in the tunnel belonged to a Fiat Uno manufactured between May 1983, and September 1989 by Seima Italiana. The white paint chips were called Bianco Corfu. When found, the car had been repainted.

to research about drugs in his blood stream.

McMoneagle - Substance review - I believe if the driver had drugs in his system, whatever kind they were, they were not there by his own hand. I have this sort of strange feeling that he was not deliberately drugged to hurt anyone, but maybe he was drugged to get the car stopped along the route for the "photographers" to get their shots. In other words, his control was tampered with by outside influences. I don't think he was drunk, possibly drugged, but not drunk.

Here the research came full circle. The paparazzi had attempted to slow the Hotel Ritz airport shuttle vehicles earlier that afternoon on the drive from the airport. Once it was discovered, Henri Paul had been an informant for domestic as well as foreign intelligence services we went back to McMoneagle. Could the British government have been involved?

McMoneagle - My sense is that MI-5 (British Intelligence) **did not put the stuff in his drink. However, one might contemplate that if he [Paul] was willing to take money from foreign intelligence operatives, he most certainly would have been open to taking money from the Paparazzi. Maybe they were hedging their bets by having a small "drink" with him in the bar before he started driving.**

And what of the high carbon dioxide levels in Dodi's blood stream? Since this viewing, there were reports of a carbon monoxide suicide in Paris that night.

McMoneagle - You have to open your perception a little bit here. He did not have to have any evidence of CO2 in his blood for them to find CO2 in a blood sample. You only have to switch the samples at the hospital, the morgue, or the lab. Or, pay off the guy who is doing the tests. You could also conceivably rig the test equipment. Also, there are drugs, which will give a false reading as well.

His being drugged enough to cause the accident could be attributed to a drug delivered in coffee, tea, or a drink beforehand. It could also have been sprayed on the inner edge of his door handle (driver's side), painted on the steering wheel, or inside a pair of driving gloves. He could have been shot with a needle delivery system, or pricked his hand, finger, leg, or almost any part of his anatomy on a delivery system getting into or out of the car. It can even be filmed across the pages of a book or map that he might have used to check directions on.

If he had a normal medical condition, they could have used a drug, which reacts violently with the drugs he is already taking for the medical condition. In which case they would either get false readings, or evidence of his medicinal drug, plus some other known drug which

would not have been viewed as culprit in the event, simply because no one recognized the possible expected reaction. You also have problems with drugs which are binary in nature and can be delivered in two sittings, so to speak, where the victim gets part A in the morning with breakfast, part B in the evening with dinner, both of which are enzymes and when mixed... cause everything from hallucinogenic behavior, to strokes.

Now we turned to what Dodi and Diana where thinking.

McMoneagle - Back seat travelers - MAJOR PROBLEM: When I try to access others who might have been in the car, I get heavy [analytic] overlay and interference as relates to Diana's death in France. My head fills up with all kinds of motorcycles, and all kinds of news... that was being broadcast about the incident. I believe there were at least two others in this target car, but digging anything out of the overlay is completely impossible.

There is a sense from the people in the back seat that they want to be alone together, but again, I then get overwhelmed with all the Princess Diana stuff... and it all runs together. So, I can't begin to tell where [the] overlay begins and real data ends. Would prefer to say nothing.

It's rather interesting. I actually have not opened the envelope nor have a clue as to the real target here; but I am being overwhelmed with overlay which is self-generated. Must have been a lot of energy around the Princess Diana stuff. Better to just go no further with it. End of Session.

An abrupt stop, on a then well-known topic, due to analytic overlay. This is a graphic demonstration of the differences between military remote viewers, storefront psychics or hot lines. The media had been saturated with Princess Diana coverage in the period between the accident and this tasking. A psychic hot-liner would have been able to talk and bill without end about what they "saw". One Operation Star Gate military remote viewer commented, "There are many "*psychics*" who have taken this type of gibberish to a finely honed skill."[xxxi] But, when McMoneagle got to the Mercedes back seat, he stopped the session. In intelligence work when you are not sure of your viewing, you must say so. Any elaboration is unethical as in life and death situations, military viewers must stay grounded in the target's realities.

Analytic Overlay [AOL] is terminology within the Controlled Remote Viewing [CRV] protocols developed by Mr. Ingo Swann for the U.S. Military Intelligence Community at the Stanford Research Institute as they developed the nomenclature. AOL can generate bad data. So, can anything be done about it?

McMoneagle - Military research - There were a number of experiments which were run to examine whether or not a remote viewer can identify "AOL" while in session. We found that it could be rarely demonstrated. Most viewers are unable to tell (accurately or consistently) when something was AOL or when it wasn't, while in session.

Facts are; Evidence produced within labs suggests that no one methodology is capable of identifying and extinguishing AOL any better than another over the long haul.

There have been significant runs of very low AOL or displays of almost no AOL which have been done by individual remote viewers. So, there are indications that some people might have a talent for producing less AOL than others. But it does not appear to be method driven since it doesn't hold up in testing across all remote viewers using the same method.

So, why should identifying AOL be important??? It is important because, while you are attempting to learn remote viewing (regardless of method), it makes you think about how and why you are "thinking" about something. It is meant to reduce the speed by which you automatically jump to a conclusion. It also supports the structure and keeps one within it (at least until one becomes proficient enough to no longer need it.)

After the impact, eyewitnesses saw a motorcycle 30 to 40 meters behind the Mercedes slow down to observe the accident and then accelerate away from the scene. At 12:26 a.m., the Paris Fire Department - Sapeurs-Pompiers Unit - received a cell phone call from a Gaelle who was in the tunnel. Within one minute another call went out to the "service d'aid medicale urgente" (SAMU) - a civilian emergency medical service.

In the wreck, Diana and bodyguard Trevor Rees-Jones were still alive. One eye witness said he heard a woman crying loudly. One of the paparazzi, Romuald Rat, indicated Diana was conscious. He claimed he told her to stay calm; that help was on the way.

Aftermath

Pandemonium broke out as the Press fought each other to get the new million dollar shot. One photographer leaned into the car to reposition Dodi's corpse for a posed picture. Someone else came with video equipment. Within five minutes, Police Officers Lion Gagliardone and Sebastien Dorzee plowed through the crowd to the car. The police report stated:

"I observe the occupants in the vehicle are in a very grave state. I immediately repeat the call for aid and request police reinforcements, being unable to contain the photographers and aid the wounded."[xxxii]

Officer Dorzee: *"I finally got to the vehicle... The rear passenger* (Diana) *was also alive... She seemed to be in better shape* (than Rees-Jones). *However, blood flowed from her mouth and nose. There was a deep gash on her forehead. She murmured in English, but I didn't understand what she said. Perhaps 'My God!'"*[xxxiii]

Ultimately, six paparazzi were held in connection with the frenzy in the tunnel. They were arrested on suspicion of involuntary homicide and failure to assist persons in danger. Excepting the 24-year-old Romuald Rat, 40 was the average age of those arrested. Twenty film rolls were confiscated providing police with the photographic evidence they needed to confirm each man's activities that night. Three paparazzi got away.

There are no Miranda rights in France, nor is there a right to call an attorney. French authorities can hold a suspect for forty-eight hours before the prisoner must be formally charged or set free. However, it is certain Henri Paul did not have to be drunk or drugged to have had an accident at that speed.

The former Princess of Wales, Diana Spencer, arrived at the Hospital de la Pitie-Salpetriere at 2:00 a.m. She was pronounced dead at 4:00 a.m. It was then she attempted to contact her son William in Scotland. "William had had a difficult night sleep and had woken many times. That morning he had known, he said, that something awful was going to happen."[xxxiv] When he was told of his mother's death he said, *"I knew something was wrong. I kept waking up all night."*[xxxv]

At 5:00 p.m. Prince Charles, 48, flew into Villacoublay military airfield outside Paris from Aberdeen, Scotland with Diana's sisters Sarah McCorquodale and Jane Fellows. "Diana's sisters spent most of the flight to Paris in tears. The Prince was controlled but clearly very shaken."[xxxvi] By 5:40 p.m. he was greeted at the hospital by the French President and Mrs. Jacque Chirac (1995-2007). Charles was led into a room with his two ex-sisters-in-laws where Diana lay in a coffin. He asked to be alone with the body for a moment. When he came out his eyes were red. The accident was 368 days after the finalization of their divorce.

Diana's coffin, draped in the Royal Standard's yellow and maroon, was flown home by an honor guard in a British Royal Air Force BAe146 military aircraft to Northolt Air Force Base in England. She was then taken to the Chapel Royal at Saint James Place.

Undertaken by Levertons, her September 6 funeral was the largest in England since the death of former Prime Minister and Nobel Literature

Prize winner Winston Churchill [1874-1965]. After the morning funeral, it was reported a million people lined the route as the body was taken from London's Westminster Abby. Different accounts estimated two to three billion people watched the day's events as the car traveled the seventy-five miles to Althorpe House. Late that afternoon her body was laid to rest on a 1,254 sq. meter (13,500 sqft) island called The Oval in a lake on the Spencer's ancestral grounds. The four hundred-year-old estate was then partially turned into a tourist attraction.

On September 9, 1997, the week after Diana was buried the Al-Fayed attorney filed civil law suits against the French periodicals *France-Dimanche* and *Paris-Match.* The complaint specified invasion of privacy with willful and wanton reckless endangerment when helicoptering "stalkerazzi" got too close over the Fayed's villa in St. Tropez. But, for the Hotel Ritz, the question became who bears responsibility for the accident? Before 1997 was out, the Fayed, Spencer, Rees-Jones and Paul families had all filed papers to be made civil parties to the investigation. Under French law, this allows them to investigate the case file and participate in any damage awards. And as for the Paparazzi's fate:

"In accordance with articles 175, 176 and 177 of the Code of Penal Procedure; The examining magistrates find that there is no case to answer in the case of the state versus the above named [Photographers]."[xxxvii]

In July, 2004 Queen Elizabeth II personally opened the Princess of Wales Memorial Fountain in the southwest corner of London's Hyde Park.

Then, in April 2008, after a three year investigation costing $7.3 million ($8.3 million/2016), a six month long British inquest report was released which included the testimony of 278 witnesses with more than 600 exhibits generating an 832 page report stating:

"Our conclusion is that, on the evidence available at this time, there was no conspiracy to murder any of the occupants of the car," Lord Stevens of Kirkwhelpington, who led the inquiry, told reporters as he presented his findings here. *"This was a tragic accident."*[xxxviii]

In September of 2012, the French magazine <u>Closer</u> published paparazzi photos of Diana's eldest son's wife Kate Middleton sunbathing topless while at the Queen's nephew, Lord Linley's French chateau. A publically released statement on behalf of the Duke and Duchess said: *"The incident is reminiscent of the worst excesses of the press and paparazzi during the life of Diana, Princess of Wales, and all the more upsetting to The Duke and Duchess for being so."*

And as for the need to use remote viewing protocols:

Evidential Details

McMoneagle - CRV (Controlled Remote Viewing) **is a "method" derived from a method the military used while attempting to "train" people to understand both protocol as well as what is going on in a remote viewer's head (such as processing or the lack thereof). It was also very specifically designed to "preclude" things from being done out of ignorance (during the RV session) that might impact on/or otherwise prevent the act of successful psychic functioning from taking place; in other words, insure that RV could be replicated and would work more times than not.**

I would add that formal testing in the SRI Lab showed that regardless of technique or methodology utilized, most viewers were unable to consistently identify AOLs when asked to identify them prior to feedback. I have to say most, because "a couple viewers" were able to do so during significant runs--but this is inherently talent based and not the general or common rule. I remind you all of what is termed the "AH-HA". If it were not for the Ah-ha's, there would not have been a program. At the end of the road, almost anything is right when you have finally come to understand that it is an inherent part of our nature and then you just simply can do it.

"We tried a lot of things. Like I always tell everyone, we "improved" on the Ingo (Swann) method a thousand times in a thousand ways. But our bottom line always had to be accuracy, so we had to keep track of the improve-ments. Most of those times, the resulting data showed that the end result of our "improvements" was to have the accuracy drop down and down and down. Those things which proved over time to work, we kept. Ingo will be the first to tell you that what we did and taught to new people coming into the unit wasn't his "pure" method. The minute someone would come back from Ingo's training, we would try to see if there were some way to make what they had learned work better in a military/political/espionage setting. Some things did work, and they are now incorporated into the "military" method which passes for the Ingo Swann method."

E-mail from former Operation Stargate Data Base Manager Lyn Buchanan - 7/29/98

What you are about to read is the data the Pentagon would have received had they tasked this event in the interests of the people of the United States of America.

The James Maybrick Material

As usual my hands are cold, my heart I do believe is colder still...And oh what deeds I shall commit.

From the "Diary" of Jack the Ripper

Visionless in a pitch black alley. Bad pay struggle with sudden throat pain. She grabbed her neck and hit the cobblestone hard on her left. But there was no time. A horse approached. The way out was blocked. Were these Jack the Rippers' thoughts?

Maybrick Diary: *I would have dearly loved to have cut the head of the damned horse off and stuff it as far as it would go down the whore's throat. I had no time to rip the bitch wide, I curse my bad luck.*[xxxix]

In May of 1991 a diary was unearthed purporting to be the private thoughts of Jack the Ripper. The so-called Maybrick Diary had emerged as a significant controversy within the Ripper community. The alleged author was James Maybrick, a cotton trader during London's 'Autumn of Terror' in 1888. Up to now (1997) researchers have had to judge from the text alone.

Unfortunately, the capability examiners failed to bring to bear was U.S. Military Intelligence strength Controlled Remote Viewing. When we targeted the murders we encountered the need to resolve the Maybrick mystery within Ripper folklore. We hoped a single "Massive Multiple Tasking" might resolve this issue.[11] So, before visiting the murder site, we targeted Maybrick's Battlecrease mansion death bed in Liverpool, England, at 8:30 p.m. May 11, 1889.

The people below are strangers to those unfamiliar with Ripper case work. But these details serve as an example of the kind of historical information available to anyone engaged in genealogical research.

Maybrick was targeted as he was expiring from arsenic poisoning at his home - and then a target was submitted for the Dutfield Yard in London's Whitechapel district eight months earlier. We waited with a sense of suspense. Was this man really Jack the Ripper?

McMoneagle - Maybrick's bedroom - I find myself inside a large room, approximately 15X18 feet. The room is located on the second floor of a blockhouse type of building--very square, very heavy, stone, or lots of plaster walls. There are heavy brocade drapes,[12] apparently earth tones, with some very dark reds, almost a black-red color running through them. Carpets are oriental. Furniture is primarily oak and some mahogany, very heavy, empire type stuff, large and ponderous. Get a sense the room is very dark or the curtains are drawn to make it dark.

---

[11] 'Massive Multiple Tasking' (MMT) is one of nine categories of tasking capabilitiess in the civilianized Controlled Remote Viewing manual as taken from the Military Protocols. It refers to the viewing of multiple events in the same session. Problems> Solutions>Innovations, 1997; General Terminology Chapter, p. 6. In this case we viewed the death scene of James Maybrick in Liverpool then moved to the Whitechapel District in London, England.

[12] Brocade is defined as, "a rich cloth with a raised design woven into it, as of silk, velvet, gold or silver." *Webster's New World Dictionary of the English Language;* College Edition; World Book Publishing.

There is a heavy sense about the room, like there is someone who is either ill, or shuns the light. There are six people who are focused on this room. One resides permanently within the room, five come and go.

James Maybrick (1838-1889) - Primary man and permanent resident: is approximately five feet, seven inches tall. Brown eyes. Moustache which droops approximately one to one point five inches downward past the crease of the lips. Light brown hair, partially bald or with a heavily receding hairline. Would say his build is about light to medium, approximately 160 pounds; medium complexion. May be (the) person who is ill or sickly.

This person was primarily a business man. I get a sense that he spent a great deal of time traveling (at least early in his career). Most of his travel was by horse drawn carriage and steamer (boat). He traded in cloth or had something to do with the haberdashery business (clothing in general). Get a sense that he was not wealthy, although the house was a nice one. He probably lived beyond his means. See him as sort of a playboy type, who probably wouldn't turn down a clandestine meeting with a pretty woman not his wife. Also get a sense that he was married. Marriage probably was not a good one.

Maybrick Diary: *My mind is clear I will put the whore through pain tonight.*"xl

He was somewhat careless with money most of his life. Get very strong feelings that he was probably careless with money because he was weak and easily influenced by outside interests-- gambling, women, drink, etc. In other words, and addictive personality type. Probably spent more time drunk than not. Have a strong sense that he blamed much of his failure in life on those around him. He was secretive and had an outrageous temper which he took out on his wife from time to time. I believe he hated his Mother, but had very little knowledge concerning his Father.

I have a strong sense that he died early from over-indulgences. Too much eating, drinking, and possibly drugs. Keep getting a vision of small vials of white powder,[13] so he may have been addicted to cocaine or heroin. May have to do with his lack of judgment with money.

See him ill for a short period of time. Severe heart problems, arrhythmias, breathing difficulties and a great deal of pain, in particular stomach pain. I believe when he died, he died very badly in a great deal of pain. Keep getting images of severe illness, unable to hold down food, severe to horrible stomach cramps, muscle aches and pain, crushing heart and chest pain, delirium, fading in and out a lot, not

---

[13] This white powder was the unusual use of arsenic as a drug.

making much sense. Did not get a very good sense about his voice, as I believe he was in the process of dying at the time. Because of his physical state...it would have sounded somewhat "coarse," or "low and dry. Died hard. Reason, probably heart failure. Of the five people going in and out, three are women and two are men.

Michael Maybrick (1841-1913)[14] - Second man: is five feet, five inches tall; Brown eyes. Much heavier...moustache with long side-burns. Darker hair (maybe dark brown or black). He weighs approximately 190 pounds and is of stocky heavy features; darker complexion. Related to Primary man.

Edwin Maybrick (1851-1928) - Third man: is approximately five feet, eight inches tall, very light framed glasses. Grey eyes, blond or very light brown hair, somewhat freckled complexion, also very heavy set, approximately 210 pounds. Also related to primary man, probably a much younger brother. Get a sense of fairly large separation in ages.

Florie Maybrick (Wife; 1862-1941) - Primary woman: Approximately five feet, six inches tall; blond hair, blue eyes; wears hair fairly long, but piled on top of her head in some kind of a roll. Fairly attractive, lightly and well built, perhaps 120 pounds. Nervous type, seems to be ill, or not feeling well. Related to Primary man as well, perhaps wife, but do not get wife type vibes, so could be sister or might be an especially close friend.

James and Florie Maybrick were married July 27, 1881. James was twenty-four years older than Florie.

Mary Cadwallader (Maid) - Third woman: Obviously an employee. Probably a maid. Approximately five feet, five inches. Much older, and stocky. About 145-150 pounds. She has black hair which she wears under some kind of a hat or scarf, dark leggings, and some kind of a two part uniform.

Alice Yapp (Nurse; b. 1860) - Second woman: Approximately five feet, six inches tall; Auburn hair, green eyes, maybe Irish. About 140 pounds, tad on the chunky side. Older than the Primary woman. Bad teeth. Get a sense she may be either distant friend of Primary man, or there temporarily for some reason. A short term job, or employed for a very specific or narrow reason. [15] The modern medical terminology

---

[14] Also known in nineteenth century English music circles as Stephen Adams, He became one of the most popular composers of his time. He also served three terms as Mayor of Ryde on the Isle of Wight.

[15] This is an interesting observation. James Maybrick had flouted his authority by hiring Alice Yapp at a time when women routinely hired domestic help. It was in this way we were able to determine it was not Nurses Wilson, Gore or Callery who also attended Maybrick.

for her role is Home Health Care provider.

McMoneagle - Was a diary was kept - Yes I believe there was, in a sense. More than one, as they were kept in series. There were small books, about 8x10 inches, with black leather covers. Approximately 75 pages in length (each volume). These books have both business as well as personal information within them. They cover meetings with people, business venture informa-tion, and thoughts regarding people other than business. Personal remembrances of his activities while overseas. I believe they were burned. Probably within a year of his death. I think the person or persons who burned them were lawyers, but not neces-sarily his own.

I believe he viewed his diaries as being personal and otherwise not open to anyone's viewing. I think he kept them only to remember certain things that had to do with business, but because he did add some personal issues to them, they were not for public access or consumption. I think he was a very secretive and private man. That may be because he had a tendency to do things that others were not supposed to be privy to -- run around on his wife, visit with houses of ill-repute, getting drunk in bawdy houses along the row of dives in town, that sort of thing.

My sense is that what I was witnessing was the fact that the primary man was dying, but not yet dead. When he died, I believe there was only one other man in the room with him and that was the "second man" (Michael Maybrick).

It has also been stated Maybrick died, "...in the arms of his 'most intimate friend', George Davidson (d. 1893)..."[xli] But this information is not documented and seems theatrical. Such were the circumstances of the death of James Maybrick of Liverpool, England. During the question session we asked:

Question: Was the person referenced above (James Maybrick) also there (Dutfield Yard Alley)?

McMoneagle – If you are referring to someone from section one (the three women and three men) my sense is no. I do not see any connection whatsoever between section one (Maybrick bedroom) **and section two** (Dutfield Yard) **of this problem. There is also no connection between Louis Diemshutz and any of the personages in section one either.**

Question: "When you viewed the dying man in the house did you get a sense if he had ever killed anyone anywhere?"

McMoneagle – No. He did not. This was a very difficult target, as it took me over three weeks to make sense out of some of it. It was shot through with what feels like layers of invented crap that really kept steering me off to one side or another. I get a sense that someone has tried to make a much larger deal over this than should be. It's as if everyone who knows about this wants to include it within all kinds of screwy ideas about a bunch of different facts that are not pertinent or do not make sense.

Just as he finally swore, in two separate affidavits, author Michael Barret's Ripper Diary was perhaps the best of the numerous Jack the Ripper hoaxes.

...the past is a chameleon that always wears a tint of the "now." It fools us into thinking it is, or always was an absolute, when, in fact, it has never been that way.

Joseph McMoneagle - *The Ultimate Time Machine*

Out, out, brief candle!
Life's but a walking shadow, a poor player
That struts and frets his hour upon the stage
And then is heard no more.

Shakespeare in *Macbeth*

Jack the Ripper

State Secret

The outrages have, in all cases, been perpetrated upon women...of a particular class: and they have been effected in each instance with a swiftness, a dexterity, a noiselessness, and, we might almost say, a scientific skill, which are, surely, very rare accomplishments in the class from which murderers are commonly drawn. Yet... we are thunderstruck at the mixture of coolness, cunning, and almost superhuman audacity with which they were achieved.

~ The London Evening Standard, 1 October 1888 ~

*Each person will form his own concept of her,
and this will be shaped by what she means to him.*

Philip Van Doren Stern

GHASTLY
MURDER
IN THE EAST-END.
DREADFUL MUTILATION OF A WOMAN.

S he was born on November 27, 1843, into the upper middleclass farm family of Beata Carlsdotter and Gustaf Ericsson in Stora (Great) Tumelhed, in Torslanda Parish, west of the port city of Goteborg (Gothenburg) Sweden. Baptized Lizbeth Gustafsdotter (Gustaf's daughter) Ericsson on December 5, she was raised with older sister Anna Christina, and two brothers Carl and Svante. Growing up, Elizabeth developed into a skinny farm girl. She was a plain Jane with big ears, kinky hair and a long neck.

Our information is that her parents had wanted a boy as their second child for farm work. As the younger of the two daughters, Liz was always in her more attractive sister's shadow. Through adolescence she wound up with the menial woman's farm chores while her older sister Anna was being brought along to do more advanced tasks. Liz did not like farm work and became a complainer to which her mother was unsympathetic. She turned lazy and shirked her responsibilities. For this her mother gradually became feed-up and was mean to her. But Elizabeth may have been taught some sewing which was common place for farm girls in the 1850's. Her mother also taught her the English language.

Before she turned two, some 650 miles (1046k) across the North Sea, the man whose judgement would play a large role in taking Jack the Ripper off the street was realizing his greatest career achievement. He was becoming the Chief Rabbi of England and Ireland, meaning he was one of the most significant European Rabbis.

On this special occasion, a congratulatory letter was received in London from New York City. The dispatch read in part: "We have received for publication the following correspondence between a committee of the Franklin Street Synagogue, New York, and the Chief Rabbi of Great Britain. Congregation Shaaray Tephillah, New York, [dated] Tebeth 13th, 5606 [1845] - To the Rev. Dr. N. M. Adler, Chief Rabbi of the British Empire.

Rev. Sir: We, the members of the Franklin Street Synagogue, in the city of New York, U. S., avail ourselves of the first opportunity to offer you our sincere congratulation on your elevation to the exalted and important office of Chief Rabbi, an office, which, in its various ramifications, affects every Israelite, be he located in the torrid or frigid zone. Permit us, reverend sir, to unite our prayer with the orisons [prayers] of your immediate flock, that Almighty God will afford you health and longevity, that the blessings of your ministry may be preserved to posterity, until the Redeemer may come to Zion...

We are, reverend sir, with profound respect, yours, earnestly, Louis Levy, Parnass, J. N. Samuel, Gabbai, [Treasurer], S. M. Isaacs, Minister of the Congregation.

In response, the newly elected Chief Rabbi from Hanover, wrote:

Evidential Details

The area known as Tumelhed in Torslanda, Sweden. In the search for Elizabeth's home, we found the surrounding land was non-tillable except for the parcel in the circle left. This is the only tract of land large enough to generate a prosperous farm life with Atlantic Ocean fishing to the west (left edge).

"...the hopes, you entertain of my ministry are highly flattering to my feeling; but you are only doing me justice in expecting that all my energies will be directed towards the conservation of our holy laws and institutions, as I otherwise should but ill discharge those sacred duties, which have been entrusted to me. In conclusion, I beg you will accept my best thanks, and most heartfelt wishes for your welfare, with which, I remain, gentlemen, Yours, very faithfully, (Louis Nathan) N. Adler, Dr., Chief Rabbi.[xlii]

And with this began the administration of the good Rabbi Dr. Natan ben Mordechai ha-Kohen Adler (1803-1890) who groomed his son to be a Chief Rabbi - Naftali (Hermann) Adler (1839-1911). Together they would face one of the greatest challenges between the Jews and the British Government since the reign of Edward I, aka. "Longshanks" [1239-1307].

At the same time the young English Queen Victoria, 24, was assuming her duties. Six years before Elizabeth was born, during her first visit to London, Victoria had taken the opportunity to acknowledge an old friend from her Ramsgate neighborhood. She now participated in her first knighting ceremony, but it was not without controversy. "The knighting of a Jew met with some reluctance among her ministers, but in her diary she wrote:[xliii]

Victoria – *I then knighted the Sheriffs, one of whom was Mr. Montefiore, a Jew, an excellent man; and I was very glad I was the first to do what I think quite right, as it should be.*[xliv] Throughout her life she repeatedly demonstrated she was a religiously open minded monarch.

In this period European trade was on the move. During Liz's youth, Goteborg emerged as Sweden's prime seaport allowing mariners to avoid sailing the Baltic Sea east to Stockholm. And since the HMS *Great Britain* (1845-1937) had been launched, iron propeller steamships were making their first appearances in world ports.

In 1848, the Queen had another religious leadership test when Irish Catholics, fleeing the potato famine, began pouring into England. In a letter to her aunt, the Duchess of Gloucester, about suffering and religious politics, she made rare comments for a Protestant ruler: "*I cannot bear to hear the violent abuse of the Catholic religion, which is so painful and so cruel towards the many good and innocent Roman Catholics.*"[xlv]

During her reign, technology would make its imprint on the world. In 1851, the first underwater telegraph cable was laid across the English Channel and a man named Singer patented a sewing machine. Herman Melville wrote his epic *Moby Dick*, and just a year earlier Titanic's Captain E.J. Smith was born. The next year, on March 30, 1852, the Queen made a journal observation about the nation's first Jewish Exchequer:

Victoria: *Mr. Disraeli (alias Dizzy) writes very curious reports to me of the House of Commons proceedings – much in the style of his books.*[xlvi] Disraeli and the Adlers would play critical roles in shaping the Queen's outlook as the Jack the Ripper case was being resolved.

Back in Sweden the increase in global commerce was so elevated that by 1856, Gotebørg, not Stockholm, became the origin for Sweden's first railroad. The vitality of the nation's second city must have been alluring to a teenage Lizbeth and it was only a day's ride from the farm. In 1859, she was confirmed in the Swedish Church which would later play a communications role in her life. But after swimming in the Kattegat Sea and seeing Gotebørg City, she realized there was more to life than being a farm wife.

As these years went by Walt Whitman wrote *Leaves of Grass* and Louis Pasteur proved that living organisms caused fermentation. And by the early 1860's, Gotebørg had become a vibrant industrial city with a population approaching 100,000. "Increased trade and shipping made it possible for Gotebørg to grow. In the eighteenth century, the town was the Swedish East India Company headquarters with a shipping line and exclusive rights to the eastern trade routes, as far as China. Tea and chinaware, the luxury goods of the period, were brought into Sweden this way"[xlvii]

With no suitors, hand me down Liz spent her last summer on the farm, and six weeks before her 18th birthday, on October 25, 1860, signed a Certificate of Altered Residence and moved to Gotebørg's Carl Johan Parish. Perhaps with an introduction through the church, she went to a nanny position caring for workman Lars Frederick Olofsson's four children.

In December of 1861, Queen Victoria's husband Albert died at age forty-two. Devastated, Victoria would morn for what became a scandalous five years in a culture that considered four to six weeks appropriate. She finally emerged for her Golden Jubilee Celebration. But this extensive grief period marked her as a depressive personality.

While the Civil War raged in America, the increasing Gotebørg port activity put recruiting pressure on the harbor brothels. There was increased demand for women to reap the mariners from the uptick in commerce. In 1861-62, Nanny Liz (age 18–19) was likely looking at the help wanted ads. There may have been one for a Swedish-English translator.

It is not clear why Liz approached a brothel. But without a suitor in the city she may have taken a position as a brothel translator in the evenings – no sex required. If this is the case, she promptly became the brothel salon's jokey little farmer's daughter virgin translator. She certainly did translating and would have had to have learned many new words. She may have even been required to enter rooms to settle Swedish - English service misunderstandings in progress.

For an impressionable young woman, there were tall tales about faraway lands. The British seafarers, sailing their new iron steamers with their innovative kerosene lanterns, telling exotic stories of India and the Orient. Months later these sailors returned with little gifts. Their worldly attitudes and mariner's naval jargon was a world apart from mid-nineteenth century Swedish farm life. Also local was the Artillerists Academy with their military chat.

Knaves. A limitless number of sailors came to Gotebørg looking for some action after months at sea. The majority were from the Swedish or British merchant marines.

This country girl's head was turned with restaurants, fashion, city nightlife and easy money. As compared to nursery work, worldly fascination, sex, cash and exotic people, while being introduced as a V.I.P. translator, all connected. She had no city friends and the brothel needed her. Plus, she had something to sell that would bring big money the first time around. Men wanting her must also have been a wonderful feeling.

During this period, Liz acquired a double life as a domestic by day and the brothel life by night. She kept her domestic job to keep up appearances. But it was risky. Starting in 1862, through 1863 and into 1864, she acquired a fastidious "double life" faculty that she would bring to a statistically

Simon's 1888 Gothenburg

Previously undetermined, here is the port of Gotebørg showing the buildings Liz knew. An educated guess puts the brothels just behind the hilly area (top left of the **black square),** off Sorliden Street on Telegraf Street. Here a series of small units dead ends into the hill. This way brothel activities were concealed from the public and the waterfront. South is the army's "Artillery Establishment" (lower left). The artillerymen could walk up the street from their Kasern (barracks) shown on the lower right.

undocumented level later in life. But she was young and carefree in an era with few gynecological, contraceptive or disease protections.

And the times were exciting. The Red Cross was formed, the speed of light measured and fellow Swede Alfred Nobel started to manufacture a liquid explosive called nitroglycerine. But leaving the Olofsson's home every evening probably became suspicious. All of a sudden she had money. On February 2, 1864 Liz initiated a residence change in Gotebørg, moving to Domkyrko by central Gotebørg's Cathedral Parish.

Then, six months after the move, in August 1964, Liz became pregnant and her world unraveled. "Those were the days when a child born out of wedlock was a bastard, pure and simple. Often the mother was abandoned by her lover, disowned by her family, and ostracized by the local community. No descent man would look at her, and her innocent child could expect to be taunted at school, sneered at in later life, and, if he was a boy, barred from certain professions."[xlviii] She was released from her nanny job.

The news went hard on her parents. Stressed and socially shamed, her mother Beata [1810-1864] died later that month, on August 25, of a chest complaint from what people said was a broken heart. Grieving and likely incensed, her father would live for another 15 years perhaps disgraced around people whom he had always had a good reputation.

Then in March 1865, the Gotebørg police registered Elizabeth as a prostitute. Before 1888, the only record of Liz's appearance was from Swedish police registry #97 identifying her as having blue eyes, brown hair, a straight nose, an oval face and a slight physical build.

Like most girls in trouble, she probably needed financial and emotional support. In those days, women generally sought remote confinement giving the baby up for adoption or to an orphanage. Pregnancy was one thing, but a police report documenting Elizabeth, of the upper class Ericsson farm family of Torslanda Parish, was a working prostitute, would have been beyond what any nineteenth farm folk could imagine. Elizabeth had brought shame and dishonour to the family's good name, and upon her mother's death was likely banished by her father with reproach and threats if she ever returned. Her last live-in boyfriend testified:

Michael Kidney - *"I thoroughly believe* [she] *...was a Swede, and came from a superior class.*"[xlix]

Nonetheless, whatever the undocumented family's twists and turns, she still had her baby for love. But on April 21, 1865, Elizabeth gave birth to a full term baby girl - still born.

Desolation. Now she had a dead baby, a dead mother, no man, no family, and perhaps no job options. She probably had debts, and the people in the brothels may have been her only friends. She started to work steady. Documents indicate that six months after losing her daughter, Liz was put on the Registry for Communicable Diseases. Admitted to a special hospital called Kurhuset (Holtermanska) for the third time by October, she reported for sequential pelvic examinations on 3, 7, 10 and 14 November, 1865.

She was diagnosed with a vaginal cancre [canker]. On the last visit, she was designated as 'Healthy' and did not have to report to the police any further. She told the authorities she was living on Philgaten Street in Ostra Haga, Gotebørg.

* * *

He was born Aron Mordke Kozmiński on September 11, 1865(?) in Kłodawa, Congress, Poland in the then Russian Empire. Every contemporary witness, including McMoneagle, estimated he was five years older.

His mother, Golda Lubnowska, was married to Abram Józef Kozmiński. Golda had turned to prostitution and Aaron was apparently a regrettable pregnancy error. History does not confirm who Aaron's real father was, but father Abram abandoned the family which included his legitimate daughters who visited Aaron's illegitimacy upon him from time to time which may be why he threatened one sister with a knife at one point.

Growing up this was apparently reinforced as his mother may have recognized the Jon that got over as the boy matured. That man was mentally ill and his mother may have known this which is why she thought spending money on Aaron was a waste. For whatever the combination of reasons, he was treated so badly he developed a burning hatred of prostitutes.

During his birth year, Liz had been an evening translator/prostitute since 1861. But now, due to having officially been on the disease registry, and in and out of the hospital, in the street vernacular she could have imaged as "dirty." She may have been the last girl to be selected in the brothel salon. That fall of 1865 she must have hit rock bottom. Nonetheless, on November 10, 1865, she started a new nanny job in the service of a Carl and Maria Wijsner of 27-29 Husargatan Street.

During her employment, a 65 Swedish Crown inheritance was released from her mother's Will through her sister. She then applied to move to Great Britain and on February 2, 1866 got approval. She decided to leave Sweden, never to return. If she had moved north to Oslo, east to Stockholm or south to Copenhagen, she could have retained some cultural familiarity within Scandinavia while also disappearing into larger cities. Had she done so, she would have melted into prostitution's great historical oblivion. But speaking English, she preferred London.

Liz knew the sailors. She may have worked a deal to travel free. She brought what belongings she could carry and turned her back on everything she had ever known. On February 7, Elizabeth took out another residence alteration certificate and set sail for London, England.[1] On July 10, she registered as a single woman and domestic servant at the Swedish Church in Prince's Square, London. An acquaintance testified she came to Great Britain:

Charles Preston - "...in the service of a foreign gentleman."[li]

And her roommate stated:

Michael Kidney - "She afterward told me she had come to England as servant to a family."[lii]

Port of Goteborg
A ship coming into port with a broken foremast. Liz's ticket/passport has not been researched. Sailing directly to England, she would have been about a week at sea.

These two accounts are likely glimpses of the same event. A foreigner could have recruited her to work for a family in London's fashionable Hyde Park area as she did have solid domestic credentials. It was also stated she had relatives on her mother's side in Britain. But she was cagey to make sure no word ever came from Sweden.

During Liz's first year in England, a cholera epidemic swept London's East End, killing 3,000 people. That same year the trans-Atlantic telegraph cable was opened for business, and Dostoevsky finished *Crime and Punishment*. In 1867, the first practical typewriter was introduced and Karl Marx published his book *Das Kapital*.

The next year Sir Anthony de Rothschild presided over the erection a new Central Synagogue on London's east end. On the 6th Nisan 5629, (March 18, 1869) the building's foundation stone was laid by Member of Parliament the Baron Lionel de Rothschild.

Once settled, Elizabeth resumed the life of a domestic. She may have wanted to leave prostitution in hopes of marrying a respectable man with a steady income. She must have worked to make her English accent authentic enough to appear British. She appeared classy and London must have been a massive attraction giving her a second chance. So it was in that upscale neighborhood, she had a relationship with a Constable. If she could marry him, she would obtain British citizenship.

Michael Kidney – "*She told me a policeman used to see her at Hyde Park before she was married to Stride.*"

Michael Kidney

But Elizabeth got pregnant again. An illegitimate child with a Bobbie meant scandal in the Victorian London police department. That kind of blot is what the Chief would like to see disappear - better yet deported. Some dedicated Ripperologist needs to unearth those personnel records. In a jam again, Liz needed to marry someone to be certain she could stay in England.

For whatever the obscure twists and turns during her first thirty-two months in London, on March 7, 1869, she married a carpenter and son of a shipwright, John Thomas Stride [1821-1884], at the Parish Church, 60 St. Giles High Street. This marriage never fit into her life's scenario, and Stride, 48, was too old to start a family. The certificate states the ceremony was performed by Reverend Will Powell and witnessed by Messers Wyatt and Tayler. She listed her address as 67 Gower Street and Stride's at 21 Munster Street, Hampstead Road, Regents Park. No photograph of John Stride has ever been produced.

Liz was now a British citizen. The marriage certificate listed her as a twenty-five year old spinster. And the marriage document betrays a desire to cut all contact with her father by changing her maiden name to Gustifson. But even more telling is that she changed her father's name from Gustaf Ericsson to Augustus Gustifson and described him not as a farmer, but a laborer living in Stockholm.[liii] This was her move to complete anonymity. This was a backlash to her father's likely accusations she had trashed the family

name which hurt her deeply. The documentation indicates there would never again be a connection with him or the Ericsson name. Now the new Mrs. Stride settled in on East India Dock Road, Poplar, safe in her citizenship.
Michael Kidney - "[She] ...*told me she was the mother of nine children.*"[liv]
That equals 6.75 years of pregnancy of which only two children were kept.

* * *

In late February 1868, Benjamin Disraeli followed the aging Earl of Derby into the Prime Minister's Office. For Queen Victoria he was a breath of fresh air compared to the previous anti-royalist crowd.

Disraeli was a writer of romance novels who's most recognizable title was *Sybil*. Before meeting with the Queen, Disraeli wrote he could, "*only offer devotion.*" It would be, he added, '*his delight and duty, to render the transactions of affairs as easy to your Majesty as possible; ...but he ventures to trust that, in the great affairs of state, your Majesty will deign not to withhold from him the benefit of your Majesty's guidance.*"[lv] When they finally met Disraeli took Victoria's hand in both of his, kissed it and said: "*In loving loyalty and faith.*"[lvi] The Queen was delighted.

Disraeli was scheduled to meet with Victoria in September, 1868. Before he departed for Balmoral, the Queen sent him a bouquet of Primrose flowers. Dictating through his wife, Disraeli responded:
Mrs. Disraeli - *Mr. Disraeli is passionately fond of flowers, and their luster and perfume were enhanced by the condescending hand which had showered upon him all the treasures of Spring.*[lvii]

Their subsequent ten day meetings went well and as he took his leave, he was presented with a box of royal family photographs and a full-length portrait of Victoria's dearly departed husband Albert.

In response to these gifts, Disraeli pointed out: "*that he could now, 'live, as it were in your Majesty's favourite scenes,'* and that Albert was, '*a gifted being' whose memory he could not recall without emotion.*"[lviii]

But on the political front, that November the Tories were defeated and Disraeli was forced to step down. When the Queen received the governmental seals back to be passed along to the incoming Liberal government, she said regretfully; "*they had never been in better hands.*"[lix]

Her September 28, 1868 journal entry said of Disraeli:
Victoria - *He certainly shows more consideration for my comfort than any of the preceding Prime Ministers since Sir Robert Peel.*[lx]

In 1869 a product called celluloid was introduced and the first suction-type vacuum cleaner was offered. Whilst over in London's Poplar District, a fiftyish John Stride could not adequately attend to the needs of a call girl growing into her thirties.

Benjamin Disraeli, 74, [1804-1881] the first Earl of Beaconsfield was elected Prime Minister twice and was the Queen's favorite. A romance writer, he charmed Victoria with his prose, devotion, and Conservative Party politics. He has a memorial in Westminster Abbey due to his brilliant service to the Empire.

EARL of BEACONSFIELD, K.C.
PHOTOGRAPHED AT OSBORNE BY COMMAND OF H M THE QUEEN.
JULY 22ND 1878
BY JABEZ HUGHES, RYDE, I.W.
ENTERED AT STATIONERS' HALL

Jabez Hughes -1878

With new lower prices, there emerged an alternative to tea. After 1850, coffee had slowly begun to make its way into British society before home brewing was available. Increasingly, commercial coffeehouses were opening around London. In these haunts' gossip, political and educational discussions, some gambling and drug dealing took place. Occasionally they were shut down by authorities.

The 1870 the London Trade Directory shows John Thomas Stride operating a coffee shop on Upper North Street in the Poplar District. He needed to retire from carpentry but it is undocumented when his coffee shop opened. The 1871 census entry shows the Strides at 178 High Street, Poplar; listed as: Family Head: John Stride, age 50, born Kent – Carpenter [not a retailer]; Wife: Elizabeth Stride, age 27, born Sweden; Visitor: Charles Thew, age 15, born Portsmouth.

Likely marginal, by 1871 Stride moved his coffeehouse to the busier Poplar High Street. And it is here that an overlooked part of Elizabeth's life emerges. It was during the early 1870's Liz told people she was working with a man she would for the rest of her life call her husband. This man was W.A. Fisher, not John T. Stride. And as a direct competitor, William A. Fisher owned a Chrisp Street coffee shop in the same district.

With similar businesses Liz made the acquaintance and then moved in with Fisher who was a step up in class from Stride. With Liz gone, John Stride hired John Dale in 1874 who replaced Liz the next year. Elizabeth's relationship with Fisher would be the closest she ever came to normal married family life. And Fisher probably taught her Yiddish.

During the 1870's Liz had two children with Fisher and they lived as common law spouses. She told everyone they were married, but there was no divorce decree, hence no marriage certificate ever issued. While they felt they simply did not need to marry, this detail would play havoc on Liz in coming years and continues to mislead Ripperologists to this day.

In 1872 Queen Victoria was informed former Prime Minister Disraeli's wife Mary Anne had died. A widower, the Queen sent her heartfelt condolences in a way that reaffirmed the bond between people who have suffered spousal death. And when in February 1874, the seventy year old Disraeli was brought back into office, Victoria was delighted. After their first meeting to discuss appointments, Disraeli kissed her hand again and said, "*I pledge my troth to the kindest of Mistresses.*" Later he told a friend:

Disraeli - *I really thought she was going to embrace me. She was wreathed in smiles, and, as she tattled, glided about the room like a bird.*[lxi]

Back at Balmoral for strategy meetings in September, Disraeli unexpectedly became bedridden with bronchitis. Against all state protocol, the Queen paid an unprecedented visit to his bedroom. At this tender bedside encounter, Disraeli is reported to have told the Queen... "'*He lives only for Her,*' he insisted, 'and *works only for Her, and without Her all is lost*'. Extravagance, Victoria understood...was part of the code of courtly love, and belonged to an age when fiction in a relationship, rather than being discreditable, only enhanced it."[lxii]

In early 1875 the Queen again sent Disraeli primroses – the flower that had been the favorite of her dear departed husband Albert, and reserved strictly for his memory. So Disraeli made it his favorite flower as well. About these flowers, he wrote Victoria of a mythical Queen Titania:

Disraeli – "*...who had been gathering flowers with her court in a soft and sea-girt isle, and had sent me some blossoms which, according to the legend, had deprived the recipient of his senses.*"[lxiii]

That November Disraeli presented the Queen with 176,000 shares [just under half] of Suez Canal stock by borrowing four million pounds through associates of the Baron Lionel de Rothschild. Victoria was ecstatic. It was exactly what the nation, the Queen, and the Foreign Secretary needed to bolster Great Britain's Middle Eastern policy.

While over on the East End, the burgeoning age of technology must have amazed people. In 1876 the first practical gasoline engine was invented in Germany. Impressionistic painters held their first exhibition and Alexander Graham Bell invented the telephone. In the States a cavalry Commander named Custer was killed at a river called the Little Big Horn.

Politically Disraeli and Victoria were getting on famously, but six weeks later, on August 11, 1876, a sickly Disraeli made his final speech in the House of Commons. The next day the Queen christened him Earl of Beaconsfield. In March 1877, the Queen asked Disraeli to sit for a portrait to be painted for her by the royal artist. She said:

Victoria – *"Lord Beaconsfield's career is one of the most remarkable in the Annals of the Empire, and none of her Ministers have ever shown her more consideration and kindness than he has. Who was now wooing whom was clear indeed."*[lxiv]

Also in 1877, the office that would bear the greatest responsibility in bringing the Ripper case to trial, the Criminal Investigation Department (CID) of the Metropolitan Police Force, was founded.

Fisher's coffeehouse was probably shut down by the authorities, and on March 21, Liz, 34, moved into the Poplar Workhouse on London's East End. How long she stayed is not clear, but she would not move back in with Stride. From the date of her marriage, to entering the Workhouse, was exactly eight years and two weeks – half of that time spent with Fisher. She clearly had a desire to be with her children, and they stayed in touch working together again. But Elizabeth is lost to history for eighteen months.

A look inside a nineteenth century English Woman's (Welfare) Workhouse. "The Workhouse should be a place of hardship, of coarse fare, of degradation and humility; it should be administered with strictness, with severity; it should be as repulsive as is consistent with humanity." - The Revd. H. H. Milman to Edwin Chadwick, 1832.

Evidential Details

* * *

"Steamer excursions were popular pastimes in the late 19th century, and the regally appointed river steamer *Princess Alice* was one of Britain's most popular excursion boats. Berthed at North Woolwich pier, the steamer regularly made day trips from London Bridge to Gravesend and Sheerness."[lxv]

"The London Steam Packet Company possessed one of the finest excursion ships in all of England, the elegantly appointed *Princess Alice*, a giant vessel with a passenger capacity of almost 800. On the warm summer morning of September 3, 1878 the excursion ship left London Bridge with more than 700 festive vacationers on board."[lxvi]

With coffee house waitressing credentials, Liz had gotten a job as a server onboard this chic Thames excursion ship. Her "husband" William also worked onboard. They were raising their children in a kind of corporate day care environment. Their personnel records have not yet been unearthed.

On this routine Tuesday evening the ship was returning to the North Woolwich Pier at about 7:40 p.m. All of a sudden, "Shouts, frantic waving of lanterns and blasts on horns did nothing to avert disaster. The collier [904 ton coal transport] *Bywell Castle* slammed into the midsection of the *Princess Alice* and literally cut the vessel in two. Hundreds of screaming children and women were dumped into the fast-moving river, none of whom had life preservers. It was all over in approximately two (to four) minutes."[lxvii] The *Princess Alice* had been struck just forward of the starboard paddle box – the hull's weakest point - which cut the ship in half

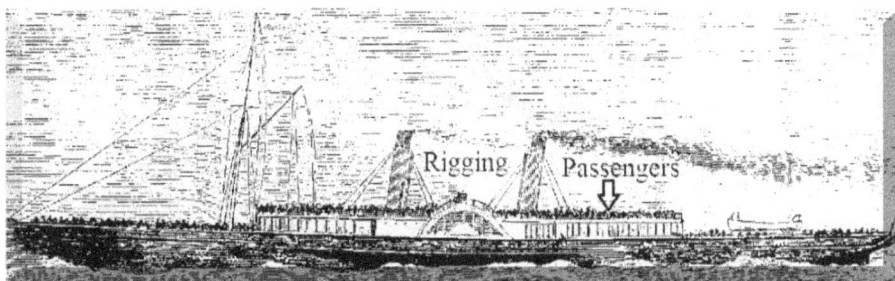

The luxury Princess Alice salon ship. While speculative, it is likely Elizabeth was serving passengers on the top deck, saw that a collision was inevitable and moved to the rigging.

During Victorian times, the Thames River was heavily polluted with a local discharge that day. The sinking was essentially into raw sewage. Estimates vary, and some died days later, but the accident killed approximately 645 of the 700 passengers and remains Britain's worst nineteenth century peacetime marine disaster. Drenched, Liz narrowly escaped death.

A newspaper artist's depiction of the *Bywell Castle* ramming the *Princess Alice* amidships. Cut in half the boat plunged to the bottom of the Thames in less than five minutes. One can imagine Elizabeth saving herself by climbing the steam funnel (rigging slightly shown middle left) as the boat quickly sank. There was just over an 8% chance she would survive this accident.

Evidential Details

As one of 55 survivors, the next day a devastated Elizabeth went to the Woolwich Dockyard where hundreds of corpses had been laid out. Picking through the remains, she identified William's and her two children's bodies. But when she attempted to claim the bodies, her identification showed the name Stride, so her claim of being Fisher's wife was rejected even though she was the only one to ID their remains.

Illustrated London News - 14 September 1878
One can imagine a horrified Elizabeth looking at the fouled corpses of her only real family. The authorities did not credit, and probably did not like, her common law wife claim.

Interestingly, Liz drew a press report stating she had witnessed her "husband" attempting to save one of her children, but that all three were drowned. Some Ripper historians have callously discounted this story as an illicit attempt to get financial assistance.

Later a "subscription" [fund] was raised for the bereaved. Liz was not allowed to apply because she was Mrs. Stride and John Stride's name was not on the West Kent Coroner C.J. Carttar's death roster. Over a decade later Coroner Baxter used this discrepancy to demonstrate that her story was fabricated. But supporting testimony does exist:

Charles Preston – *"She told me she had been married, and that her husband was drowned at the foundering of the Princess Alice. I have some recollection... [she] told me her husband was (had been) a sea-faring man."*[xviii]
Michael Kidney – *"She also told me her husband had kept a coffeehouse at Chrisp Street, Poplar, and that he was drowned on the Princess Alice." "Two [children] were drown on the Princess Alice with her husband, and the remainder are in a school belonging to the Swedish Church. I have also heard her say that some friend of her husband had two of the children. Both (of her) deceased [children] and her husband were employed on board the Princess Alice."*[xix]

Evidential Details

<u>Sven Olsson</u> – [Swedish Church Clerk] *"She told me her husband was drowned on the Princess Alice.*
<u>Coroner</u> – *"Have you any* (children's) *schools connected with the Swedish Church?"*
<u>Sven Olsson</u> – *"No; I do not remember hearing she had any children. She told me her husband went down in the Princess Alice.*[lxx] Mr. Olsson is the church clerk by which Liz communicated with her sister in Sweden.

On October 8, 1888, The *Manchester Guardian Evening News* ran a story quoting the Woolwich newspapers. The paper indicated a woman named Elizabeth Stride was a witness at the Inquest claiming her husband died in the tragedy. She never stated that husband was John Stride. But a W.A. Fisher, and their two children, had drowned in the disaster.

Liz told authorities she avoided drowning by climbing the ships funnel rigging. She further claimed she was accidentally kicked hard in the mouth by a retired police arsenal inspector struggling above her on the "companionway." This had knocked teeth out along the side of her mouth. But, certain authors have discounted something as solid as the lost teeth indicating there was no apparent problem with the hard or soft palate in her mouth. But this was about missing teeth.

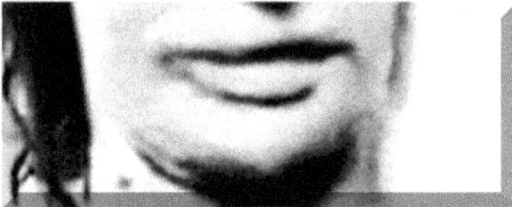

After more than ten years of healing, Elizabeth's mouth still showed the effects of the Princess Alice tragedy.

<u>Elizabeth Tanner</u> – *"She told me she was a married woman, and that her husband and children went down in the ship Princess Alice."*
<u>Coroner</u> – *"Are you sure it is her?*
<u>Elizabeth Tanner</u> – *"I am quite sure. I recognize the features, and by the fact that she had lost the roof of her mouth. She told me that happened when the Princess Alice went down."*[lxxi]

Those that discount the event have failed to explain why Elizabeth even crossed the Thames to return to the Woolwich Dockyard, and why she identified these particular bodies. It is unknown why anyone would claim two children's corpses if they weren't known to them. It is also unclear why a Woolwich newspaper would report a woman named Stride had identified her husband and children bodies if it never happened. Ripperologists need to admit that for years Elizabeth was the common law wife of W.A. Fisher. Their corpses were buried in Woolwich Cemetery's 120 person common grave as unclaimed.[lxxii]

With this new calamity, Elizabeth's life now collapsed a second time. She had already suffered the loneliness of a stillborn, the loss of her childhood home, family, and all she knew in Sweden. Now, she suffered grief and loneliness after watching the only man she could really call a husband, with the only children she ever raised, all perish in a freak accident. She must have been horrified coming upon their wet, bedraggled blueish corpses.

All that she had worked for in terms of family had vanished. The only two children that knew their mother were gone. The fact that no one else came to claim Fisher's body should have had a bearing on authorities. But Liz was dismissed as merely out to hustle a stipend which surely added insult to injury. She had no say about their being put into the common grave. But we did learn that all unknown victims were photographed and possessions kept before they were buried. Authorities stated, "…in consequence of the danger to health it was found necessary to bury many bodies unidentified." Those photographs need to be located.

And so once again no one in the world cared about Elizabeth. She was alone, with no job, a children's household that had to be peddled, with severe, untreated dental pain. She would chew on one side for the rest of her life. Her face was aged by this trauma. And as her thirty-fifth birthday neared, her mouth emerged as worse affliction than anything in Sweden. It was the kind of facial jinx that makes men move on, or treat her as a beater for cheap. And that is what happened. No longer lovely, Liz sank deeper into a now middle aged, less desirable, anything goes, rough stuff, street walking hooker, which is very different than the protection of a brothel salon. That may be the reason an earring was ripped from her pierced ear that the coroner's report noted had since healed.

After the *Princess Alice*, a destitute Liz went back to John Stride now age 60. This time they must have lived together at least two years as the 1881 census shows John and Elizabeth Stride living at 69 Usher Road, Bow. There were no declared children after 12 years of "marriage."

* * *

The month before the *Princess Alice* tragedy, the Salvation Army was formed at 272 Whitechapel Road. In politics, Benjamin Disraeli was in Germany negotiating a settlement to Russo-Turkish tensions in the Middle East. War was avoided and Disraeli negotiated control of Cyprus for the British Empire. Having already extended him the Order of the Garter, an impressed Queen wrote:

Victoria – *"Would he not accept a Marquisate or Dukedom in addition to the Blue Ribbon? And will he not allow the Queen to settle a Barony or Viscounty on his Brother and Nephew? Such a name should be perpetuated!*[lxxiii] But many took a dim view of extending these tributes to a Jewish family.

Sometime in 1879, likely through church clerk Sven Olsson, Liz heard that on February 6, her father Gustaf [1811-1879] had died. She had not seen him for fourteen years and one can only guess at the ambivalent feelings this brought on.

During this period the industrialized democracies standard of living was pulling away from the rest of the world. In 1880, the first water borne frozen meat shipment was transported from Australia to England. The British opened the world's first public electrical power station in Godalming, and the Royal Albert Dock opened on the Thames River.

Eliminating serfdom in Russia, the progressive Tsar Alexander II (1818-1881) was assassinated by Marxists revolutionaries in March. The anti-Jewish backlash led to the May Laws of 1882 putting new restrictions on Jewish liberties. Poland had been under Russian rule since the uprisings of 1863. Between 1881 and 1920 some two million Jews left the Russian Empire. Moving to Germany and then on to London, England in 1881, some of the Kosminski's made this move.

As Prime Minster Disraeli's term came to an end, Parliament was dissolved and from Downing Street he wrote to Victoria in the third person.
Disraeli – *Lord Beaconsfield, no longer in the sunset, but the twilight of existence, must encounter a life of anxiety and toil; but this too, has it's romance, when he remembers that he labours for the most gracious of beings."*[lxxiv]

After elections that brought the Liberal Party back into power, Queen Victoria wrote to Disraeli:
Victoria - *What your loss to me as a Minister would be, it is impossible to estimate. But I trust you will always remain my friend, to whom I can turn and on whom I can rely. Hope you will come to Windsor in the forenoon on Sunday, and stop all day, and dine and sleep.*[lxxv] Lord Beaconsfield wrote back that his relations with her:
Disraeli – *"...were his chief, he might almost say his only happiness & interest in this world."*

In return, the Queen requested that he write to her in the extremely privileged first person tense, indicating that:
Victoria – *"when we correspond, which I hope we shall on many a private subject & without anyone being astonished or offended, & even more without anyone knowing about it—I hope it will be in this more easy form ....You must not think it is a real parting. I shall always let you know how I am & what I am doing, & you must promise me to let me hear from you & about you."*[lxxvi]

Benjamin Disraeli left Downing Street for the last time on April 25, 1880. He would continue to correspond and was the only former Prime Minister to stay in Windsor Castle for a total of three times that year. In her private journal, the Queen wrote:

<u>Victoria</u> – *"I then took leave of him, shaking hands, when he kissed mine. I would not consider this as leave taking...and that I begged he would always let me know his whereabouts so that I could always give him news of myself."*[lxxvii]

After this, Disraeli's health deteriorated. He had his last dinner at Windsor on March 1, 1881. Pulmanological ailments plagued him and even the Royal specialist in chest diseases could not save him. He died on April 19. In her journal, she wrote:

<u>Victoria</u> – *"Received the sad news that dear Lord Beaconsfield has passed away. I am most terribly shocked and grieved, for dear Lord Beaconsfield was one of my best, most devoted, and kindest of friends, as well as wisest of counsellors."*[lxxviii]

Again the Queen grieved so much she could not attend his funeral. She brooded and asked if Disraeli could be buried at Westminster Abbey. Two months later, on April 30, she journeyed to see his casket and then to sit in his library. As she sipped tea she later recalled in her journal:

<u>Victoria</u> – *"I seemed to hear his voice, and the impassioned, eager way he described everything."*[lxxix]

Back on London's east end, Elizabeth was admitted to the White-chapel Infirmary for a whole week on December 28 suffering from bronchitis, a similar ailment to Disraeli's.

On April 19, 1882, the Queen sent primroses to Disraeli's grave.

<u>Victoria</u> – *"I sent a wreath of them to place on the grave of my dear and even more missed and regretted friend Lord Beaconsfield today—the first anniversary of his death."*[lxxx]

Also that year, Liz moved to common housing at 32 Flower and Dean Street rather than stay with Stride any longer. Her life was about to take another turn. Just as the first cash registers started to appear in English retail stores, "All the evidence tends to indicate that Elizabeth Stride was leading something of a double life from, at least, the beginning of 1882."[lxxxi]

Working with tailors and learning to sew, Liz had happened onto a seamstress named Mary Malcolm. She probably reminded Liz of what she projected her older sister looked like some eighteen years on. And Liz reminded Mary of her long lost sister Elizabeth Stokes. Somehow these women "recognized" each other as actual "sisters" and Liz went along.

In March 1883, the Jewish community suffered the sudden death of their beloved Minister A. L. Green. In February 1884, the Rev. E. Spero of the Hambro Synagogue was elected Reader and in July, Bristol's Rev. D. Fay was elected Preacher. Also that year Liz moved in with waterside laborer Michael Kidney [b.1852], at 35 later 36 Devonshire Street.

Evidential Details

In the year the steam turbine was invented, John Thomas Stride died of heart disease on October 24, 1884, age 63. He was living at the Poplar Union Workhouse, but died at the Sick Asylum in Bromley. Liz's formal marriage was now dissolved.

In 1885, the Eastman Kodak Company introduced the first commercial film and aluminum was introduced for commercial use. And for the Queen's depressive disposition, on April 19, she wrote:

Victoria – "*The anniversary of dear Lord Beaconfield's death. Oh! Were he but still alive!*"[lxxxii] *Primrose Day! Already five long years since good Lord Beaconsfield* [Disraeli] *was taken.*[lxxxiii]

Sigmund Freud: "*The neurotic ceremonial consists of little prescriptions, performances, restrictions, and arrangements in certain activities of everyday life which have to be carried out in the same or in a methodically varied way.*"[lxxxiv]

As England moved into a new era of business respectability, critical changes developed in how the law was to be administered. In 1870, Parliament had passed the Prosecution of Offenders Act creating the Office of Director of Public Prosecutions as appointed by the Home Secretary. An 1879 bill resulted in the setup of the1880 Public Prosecutions Office. Then a follow-up Bill in 1884 was called the Prosecution of Offenses Act. This legislation further removed prosecutors from police investigations.

The police were to apprehend criminals and provide evidence to this new Prosecutions Office who would decide which charges were to be preferred. After a slow start, the former Treasury Solicitor, Augustus K. Stephans (1827-1904) was installed. Aggressive and no nonsense, he was a fine choice as he had prosecuted civil and criminal cases at the Admiralty, the Works Office, Her Majesty's Proctor's Office and the War Office.

The new Director of the Public Prosecutions Office for England and Wales (1884-1894) assumed responsibilities for all capital cases, as well as counterfeiting, bankruptcy offenses, corporate fraud and served as the legal department for all governmental administrations in the London Metropolitan area. From 1880 to 1889, the caseload moved from 500 to 1300 per year. "It was a workload which reflected not only the prosecutorial energy but the changing priorities of the late Victorian criminal justice system."[lxxxv]

What Ripperologists have failed to see is that the energetic Stephens certainly possessed the facts in a case as high profile as Jack, and was prepared to prosecute. But the fact is Stephens is not in Ripper literature and his career details are obscure.

He was probably angered over Kosminski's ability to circumvent justice and so was brought more deeply into the system. In 1889, as Jack was being interned at an insane asylum, Stephans was elevated to Queen's

Counsel while also a Director, meaning he received two incomes. Any case file, assembled in preparation for the Ripper's prosecution, has vanished.

In May, 1886 Liz listed her address as Devonshire Street with the Church while applying for financial assistance. She lived with Michael Kidney the next three years but, independent, she tended to drift away when she pleased. She was not in love and their relationship could be stormy.

Michael Kidney – *"She was subject to going away whenever she thought she would. During those three years I have known her she has been away from me altogether about five months. It was drink that made her go away, and she always returned without my going after her. I have cautioned her the same as I would a wife."*[lxxxvi]

The nine years younger Kidney attempting the role of husband did not suit Liz, and their quarrels became violent probably over prostitution, finances, and drunkenness. Elizabeth then charged Kidney with assault, the arrest being made by Police Badge 357H. But Liz knew he cared, and failed to appear before the Thames Magistrates Court. The charges were dropped on April 6, 1887.[lxxxvii] But this may have been because she too was in trouble with the law. She was increasingly drunk and disorderly.

* * *

In June, 1887, another Polish immigrant named Israel Lipski (nee Lobulsk) [1865-1888] employed Harry Schmuss and Henry Rosenbloom in his umbrella stick business at 16 Batty Street, London. Hand engraved umbrella handles were in demand and costly. Lipski found a way to use acid engraving to reduce the production time of his very competitive product.

On June 28, police were summoned to recover a woman's body in a Stepney doss house off Commercial Road. They found a six month pregnant woman named Miriam Angel with yellow staining around her mouth. Her death was determined to be by the ingestion of nitric acid. Authorities also found Israel Lipski, 22, hiding under her bed barley alive with the same yellow staining around his mouth.

Mr. Lipski spoke little English. He admitted to recently purchasing nitric acid for his business. But it had been used to kill Ms. Angel and he was charged with her death. He was subsequently convicted of first degree murder and sentenced to hang.

Lipski steadfastly maintained his innocence claiming she had been murdered by Schmuss and Rosenbloom who thought they had already killed him by forcing acid into his mouth. What is likely is these two men saw promise in Lipski's business and decided to take it by killing him and the unfortunate witness. Killing Ms. Angel would make it look like a murder suicide, but the crime was botched when Lipski was found alive.

However, in the street it looked like the murder of a woman carrying Lipski's baby. Anti-Semitism boiled over during the trial and street fights broke out. During the days leading up to the execution, a Rabbi Singer repeatedly visited Lipski in prison. Then, on the day before his death, Lipski allegedly confessed his guilt to the Rabbi. "Was he persuaded that confession might somehow help his people, his family or himself? Did he confess to shield someone or in the hope of a last minute pardon?"[lxxxviii]

Being of the faith, Lipski apparently agreed to cover the crimes of his former partners to end the police scrutiny based on his sworn court accusations. One death in the community was enough. Whatever the details, Rabbi Singer would have kept Rabbi Adler appraised. Even though he was innocent, Lipski had become a Jewish community imaging problem.

Shocked that his migration to England had ended this way, he died in the Newgate Prison yard on August 21. Public disdain was so strong that on the day of his hanging people gathered at the prison to cheer. But the execution of an innocent Jew brought a scornful and distrustful community reaction against the police and the British justice system in general.

Did these same generation polish immigrants – Aaron and Israel - meet at Central Synagogue? That is unknown but, as the innocent and sympathetic Israel Lipski dropped 13 feet through the trap door, he could not have known he gave his life so Jack would live.

* * *

As life moved into 1888 nothing much changed for Elizabeth. She turned 44 on November 27, 1887 and was likely undergoing a difficult menopause without pharmacy. Cleaning, soliciting the pubs, and then back to her shared apartment with Michael, she probably became alcoholic. She was apparently not happy living with Kidney or with life in general. She was negative because she realized her prospects were bad.

As the winter months were ending, remarkable crimes appeared in the headlines. On February 25, an Annie Millwood was admitted the Whitechapel Workhouse Infirmary with multiple stab wounds to her lower body and legs. She was released on the 21st of the next month but died ten days later. A witness to a knife attack against a woman's pelvis was gone.

As February moved into March, the rainy London winter ran its course, and Liz continued her "sisterly" encounters with seamstress Mary Malcolm. They had become close due to their weekly meetings over five years. Elizabeth had always wanted the love of family. Now she was involved with a stranger with whom she was able to carry out what doctors agree is the ultimate human game – foreign language sibling impostering.

These women's conversations likely referenced the news. During the night of March 27-28, a man came to the 39-year old Ada Wilson's door, demanded money and then stabbed her twice in the throat. Though her wounds were considered mortal, she nonetheless was released a month later. Her assailant was never caught.

Then, on April 3, a woman named Emma Smith was sexually assaulted, raped and left to die by three men on London's East Side. Violent outdoor gang rape was unusual even on the tough side of town and made news. She died the next day and another woman was dead with three murderous attacks in six weeks. The public started to notice.

Through the summer of '88, Elizabeth was drinking earlier in the day and was threatened with incarceration if she did not stop her Court appearances on drunk and disorderly charges. She had become a loud, irate, snaky drunk. Charles Preston had known Liz for almost six years.

Charles Preston - *"I have known her to be in custody on one Saturday afternoon for being drunk and disorderly at the Queen's Head public house, Commercial road. She was let out on her own bail on the Sunday morning."*[xxxix]

The spring and summer of 1888 ran its course like this. During that summer William Burroughs invented a mechanical adding machine, and Mrs. Benz was the first woman to ride 66 miles in her husband's "motor wagon". But years of cleaning by day and drinking by night blurred. Turning tricks became more uncertain and what the men wanted more debauched.

That fall she was pushing forty-five years old. She probably used alcohol to cope with life. The mirror told its tale of a doubtful mouth and the decline in her beauty. "She appeared eight times on drunk and disorderly charges at Thames magistrate's court..."[xc] in twenty months. Eight times in less than two years is an appearance every 2.5 months. Liz finally threw herself at the Court's mercy pleading "feminine hysteria." Another time she told the court she was an epileptic to avoid jail time.

Mary Malcolm – *"I believe she has been before the Thames Police-court magistrate on charges of drunkenness. I believe she has been let off on the ground that she was subject to epileptic fits, but I do not believe she was subject to them. ...unfortunately drink was a failing with her. I have never seen [her] ...in an epileptic fit – only in drunken fits."*

Coroner – *"Have you ever heard she was in trouble with any man?"*

Mary Malcolm – *"No, but she has been locked up several times. She has always been fined and the money has been paid.*[xci] Probably by Kidney.

Then on August 7, a vicious murder took place in Whitechapel. The body of a thirty-nine year old part time prostitute named Martha Tabrum [1849-1888] was found on the first floor landing in an apartment building in George Yard. She had been stabbed 39 times in the neck and torso with three different knives. Some think this was Jack experimenting with blades.

At the Inquest Deputy Coroner George Collier said, *"The man must have been a perfect savage to inflict such a number of wounds on a defenseless woman in such a way."*[xcii] There were no solid leads and London's East Enders were left wondering if anyone in the previous murders was involved.

Then, just three weeks later, a forty-three year old prostitute named Mary Ann (Polly) Nichols [1845-1888], was found dead in Bucks Row.

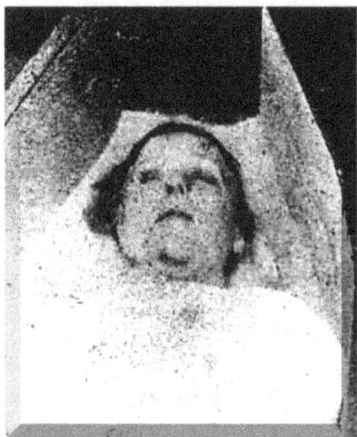

Bruises on her face indicated the victim's head had been steadied in a struggle before her throat was slit down to the vertebrae. Then her abdomen had been cut deeply three or four times. Analysis indicated the murderer had lingered for up to five minutes and exhibited extreme violence.

Polly Nichols had been sliced up right on a city sidewalk. London's press started to cry out for action to apprehend what was a blood thirsty killer. Horrified with the coroner's details, the press wondered aloud if these murders were connected. Women started to get indoors before dusk.

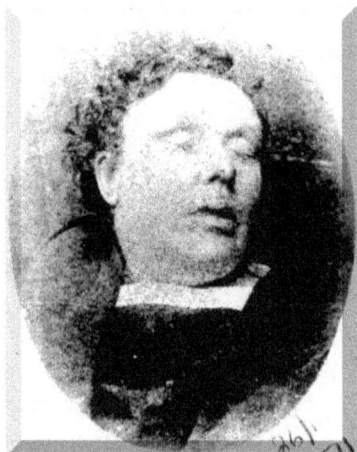

In this charged atmosphere, the next weekend of September 8, forty-seven year old Annie Chapman [1841-1888] was found butchered at 5:30 a.m. An Elizabeth Long testified she saw the victim outside #29 Hanbury Street with a man in a dark coat that looked Jewish and sounded like a foreigner. They went through a passageway to the backyard minutes later.

Chapman was seized by the chin and strangled. Bruises indicated her jaw was held in place as her throat was slit. Doctor Phillips surmised the attack was so savage as to have twice attempted to remove her head. This was due to cuts on the spine's left side moving inward. The attacker then turned to the body.

Again, the intestines were opened but this time they were removed and placed above her right shoulder. The assailant removed the ovaries, upper part of the vagina and two thirds of her bladder. These organs were removed and never recovered. Dr. Phillips speculated the knife was a 6 to 8 inch thin blade weapon. With Chapman's murder the community realized a knife-wielding psychopath was at large in Whitechapel.

Shocked, the public viewed this as four vicious attacks on women in six months, with a bold and cunning fiend now raising the anti to two in seven days. An obsessed butcher, who risked apprehension carrying smelly blood evidence, was walking the neighborhood. At this point the public started to panic and formed their own Whitechapel Vigilance Committee. Intense pressure was put on police to apprehend the murder. But each time the man who became Jack the Ripper vanished without a trace.

With this as a backdrop, Michael Kidney and Liz were quarrelling again as Kidney probably became troubled about more drunken incarceration fines. Living together became so difficult through September, that on Thursday the 27th, Liz walked out and checked in at 32 Flower and Dean Street. It was the first time in three months. Catherine, wife of Patrick Lane and also a resident, said Elizabeth moved in mid-week because of a fight. Catherine Lane - *"I spoke to... [Liz] on Thursday between 10 and 11 in the morning. She told me she had a few words with the man she was living with and left him."*[xciii] She had stayed with Michael Kidney all September until that last Wednesday. But if they fought, Kidney later refused to confirm it.

After the James Maybrick remote viewing, McMoneagle was requested to move backward in time to Whitechapel's Dutfield Yard entrance on September 30, 1888 just before 1:00 a.m. The weather in London had been rainy and mild. Elizabeth was talking to a man on a Berner Street sidewalk. Perhaps due to the public outcry, the Ripper had not struck for three weeks and people had become a little less vigilant. Looking her in the face...

McMoneagle - Elizabeth's appearance - She has what I would call a long face, meaning longer than wide. Not pretty, but not ugly either--more of run of the mill. I believe there is something wrong with her jaw as it is kind of cockeyed--doesn't line up with her upper mouth area. I've not seen anything related to a broken jaw, but her teeth on one side were either heavily damaged or missing...double chin, jaw is narrow but square on the end, heavy skin padding over the cheek bones.

She has a long and thin nose, light eyes--gray or light blue, hair is auburn or dark brown with some reddish streaks outward away from

her head, dark bags and circles under her eyes, longer neck than usual, and thin. Hair is long ...dark brown, probably auburn color hair (light reddish tint to it); Believe she was wearing her hair up at the time, tied in some fashion either with a scarf or pinned and then covered with a scarf. Approximately five feet, five inches tall; very pale complexion -- as if she spends most of her time in doors.

Elizabeth Stride, the middle aged cleaning lady farm girl hooker. This is believed to be a death mask rendering by a police artist.

True to her background, on Saturday afternoon Liz cleaned the boarding house's rooms, earning six-pence from Lodging House #32 Deputy Elizabeth Tanner. Later a kindly Mrs. Tanner said, "...*a better hearted, more good natured, cleaner woman never lived.*"[xciv]

McMoneagle - I believe she was down on her luck, a rather sad person, living hand to mouth, pessimistic, droll [possessing an odd quality; amusing in a quaint way]**, and not particularly liked by others, which essentially wasn't her problem actually. Just all around an unfortunate soul.**

* * *

"Some have seen him as an embittered émigré, living in a fantasy world of revolutionary cliques, [others] ...as a fervent Hebrew prophet denouncing oppression, injustice, and the cash-nexus while heralding the inevitable coming of the Kingdom of Man."[xcv] He would go on to influence practically every foreign policy decision in the Twentieth Century. As a direct result of his works, more than 100 million people perished while close to another half billion would be uprooted for "re-education" or resettlement. Yet only eleven people attended his funeral.

The year after the death of "social philosopher" Karl Marx on March 14, 1883, an organization called the International Workers Educational Club was founded in London's Whitechapel district. Leveraging their money, they bought a building located across the street from the London School Board building. It was a three story structure in front of the Dutfield Yard. The building was, "Acquired in 1885 by Jewish Socialists, it became one of the favoured centres for immigrant anarchists and intellectuals, especially following its acquisition of the influential newspaper *Arbeter Fraint.*" [*The Workers Friend*][xcvi]

Founded by Morris Winchevsky [aka Leopold Benedikt] the newspaper was London's periodical dedicated to fostering Marxism revolution. It was edited by Philip Kranz[16] and printed by William West. The club members took over the paper's production in June, 1886 upgrading it from a monthly to a weekly. The paper originated from the Dutfield Yard. Along one side of the yard was a brick building housing the newspaper. Lengthwise down the club's side was an alleyway leading to the open air work yard.

McMoneagle – Alleyway - Get an image of a narrow stone or brick lined hallway or passageway--could be a tunnel. It is very dark and there are no lights. There is a smell of urine, feces (animal and human) [there were outhouses across from the building]. **Damp, like there is a coating of water on everything. Might be raining, but may also be moisture from heavy dew. There are heavy wooden doors to this tunnel** (alleyway), **but they are open. Get a sense they open outward versus inward, are very heavy, made from rough, thick boards.**

Dutfield Yard – [Passageway]…opens out into some kind of an inner area with an opening in the roof. Get a sense of animals to one side, maybe open stalls. Maybe inside a barn with a bad roof. Small rooms for some kind of storage or working areas along one side, and the back wall of a large building that sort of melds into the side of the barn. Ground is primarily brick set in sand or dirt. Old area, not fully used, or partially abandoned. Lots of bird shit everywhere, so there may be a lot of chickens or pigeons all over the place, inside and outside the buildings. Buildings are very old (circa 1750 – King George II). **So, it is either a very large barn with a large segment of roof missing (damaged); or it is an actual open court yard with many interlocking shed type roofs all converging across the space nearly enclosing it. The floor of this place is stone (cobblestones).**

By 1888, membership had grown. On September 29, the Whitechapel membership was gathering for their Saturday night meeting at 40 Berner Street. Chairing the evening's proceedings was a Russian immigrant jewelry dealer named Morris Eagle of #4 New Road. He was the evening's speaker charged with firing up the crowd to reinforce their loathing of the bourgeois. Mixed with alcohol, it was a virulent mix for someone with a hatred of prostitutes. That night the 200 capacity club hosted 90–100 mem-

---

[16] Ukrainian Jacob Rombro [1859-1922] changed his name to Philip Krantz and moved to the USA in 1889 to spread Marxism editing the American Marxist newspaper the *Arbeter Zeitung.*

bers most of whom departed between 11:30 and midnight. Afterward 20 to 30 members stayed to drink into the morning.

MORRIS EAGLE

"The yard (alley) in which the body was found is about ten feet wide. The width is continued for a distance of eight or ten yards, at which point there occurs on the left-hand side, a small row of (out) houses, which are set back a little, so that the width is increased by two feet or more. The extreme length of the court is 30 yards, and it terminates in a workshop."[xcvii]

McMoneagle - Get a sense of noise, voices, drunken laughter coming from someplace nearby; maybe a bar or drinking establishment. Have a sense that it might be some kind of a gaming/social club sort of hang-out nearby.

What makes the Stride case unique is the myths built up around her, and the people claiming to have seen Liz with a man that night. Aside from people who testified they saw nothing suspicious at critical moments, conflicting and coinciding claims are made by several observers over a two hour period on the night in question.

Time will not be wasted with grocer Matthew Packer's [1830–1907] grapes sold to the Ripper yarn. His reward money claim is not a "legendary" component of the story. His evolving statements were so misleading he was not even requested to appear at the Inquest. His "...detail about the grapes appears to have been a baseless fiction."[xcviii] However, in an effort to be thorough, we went back and submitted two word identification questions. McMoneagle was asked if these words pertained to the target.

McMoneagle - Word associations - Socialist = believe this might also be connected to the place he [Diemshutz] went for help. Grapes = no connection to anything at all.

The reason Louis Diemshutz stated Elizabeth was tightly clutching grapes in one hand - sweets in the other[xcix] was to cast some false light. The police did not find grapes, but Packer had claimed it, so Diemshutz ran with it to introduce uncertainty.

A Russian photographer/printer visiting London from the States, Joseph Lave, was living at the IWEC clubhouse. He told police he saw a "stranger" that night who said he was a Polish barber from George Yard. Not an Englishman, he later realized he had provided good information, and later claimed the man was Russian.

Another traditional Berner Street murder image is the doctor's shiny black Gladstone bag. Mrs. Fanny Mortimer of 36 Berner Street, told the

London *Daily News* she saw a man with this type of bag walk quickly by and turn the corner across from the Dutfield Yard entrance. What the press did not report later was that this man turned out to be Leon Goldstein, an IWEC member. He was cleared when he voluntarily identified himself to police as the man with the bag that contained empty cigarette boxes.[c]

Because of the amount of cutting on the other Ripper victims, speculation abounded the Ripper was medically knowledgeable. Countless illustrators and self-proclaimed "historians" have ballyhooed the Gladstone bag until such time as it was institutionalized into the movies becoming an integral part of the public's imagination. Such are the images originating from Elizabeth's involvement.

* * *

Liz's whereabouts before 11:00 p.m. that night have not been established. What is known is that she ate and drank at a bar called The Bricklayers Arms on Settles Street, some five blocks or 500 yards (.457K) away from the IWEC building.

McMoneagle - Liz's evening - I believe the woman met a man in a pub or drinking establishment earlier. They drank together and got pretty well sotted. She was probably drinking a kind of very sweet something. I get a sense of something like wine, sugar, and liqueur mixed together, then heated. I believe they did their drinking and eating in a Pub, which was distinctly different from the meeting hall area (IWEC). They left the establishment through a rear door, and proceeded through the...area looking for a place to have sex, or at least this was on the mind of the woman. Her last meal was a combination plate of cheese, potatoes and a "farinaceous" powder.

Messers John Gardner and J. Best both saw Elizabeth leaving Bricklayers as she hesitated before going into the rain just after 11 p.m. After eating something for a base to drink on, Liz had to get on with this man, as she knew of a meeting nearby that would be adjourning soon. She was with a man, "...about 5'5" tall with a black moustache, weak, sandy or missing eyelashes, and wore a morning suit and billycock hat. He was definitely English."[ci] Clearly nationality and foreign accent questions had become a part of the investigation.

McMoneagle - Ripper's voice - I would say that he has a deeper voice than not. It would be what one would call "rough sounding," or "coarse." I also believe he had an accent, but not an English accent. Do not get a good enough perception to say... He is foreign, with an accent.

Frequently the hookers of the day had sex outdoors by bending forward and putting their hands on their knees. This was because neither party could afford a room. The Dutfield Yard was a perfect place for such encounters as it was pitch black, semi-private, and the heavy wooden gates were generally open. "Here from a distance of some eighteen feet from the street, anyone entering the yard had to pass between the dead walls of Nos. 40 and 42. Here, after sunset, the darkness was almost absolute."[cii] In fact, there were only four flickering lamps on Berner Street between Commercial Road and Fairclough Street.

Liz knew her audience and had to be ready for some rough stuff. She was in a bad neighborhood looking classy. Witness Charles Letchford said: *She had on a black alpaca dress, a black jacket trimmed with fur, an old velveteen bodice, once black but now brown, and a crape bonnet, some spare space in which had been filled up by a newspaper, white stockings, white stays, and side spring boots.*[ciii] She came complete with a communist red flower backed by a maidenhair fern on her breast, which added the correct color coordination to a downright bourgeois image.

That night she was soliciting the monthly IWEC meeting of fired up Bolshevik revolutionaries. A beer hall full of exhorted and potentially violent revolutionary drunks was the kind of work most girls would avoid. But of the type of womanhood a Marxist would want to take in an alley, the sexual degradation of an upper class middle age woman, was the perfect hook.

Previously events leading up to Stride's death had been puzzling. In other rippings, the victim left to find a customer and was not seen alive again. But in this case, Elizabeth was met by many men coming and going from the club and she stayed in the area for approximately two hours.

Because time pieces were still primarily for the well to do, any statement about the comings and goings of the people on Berner Street that night can be challenged. However, this stalking scenario seems to explain this puzzle as plausibly as anything previously published.

Sometime before 11:30 p.m., Elizabeth concluded her business with the man on Settles Street. She proceeded to the IWEC building on Berner Street aware the meeting would be adjourning soon. The set-up was perfect for sex because of the Dutfield Yard behind the building. From the front of the building she could monitor the front and side exits.

Just before 11:45, a stout man (Jack) propositioned Liz in front of the IWEC. She walked the man south past Fairclough Street and down Berner [now Henriques] Street with his arm around her for some of the time. He may have even kissed her, but Liz does not want to get involved. From his front door, ink warehouse laborer William Marshall, of 64 Berner Street, saw the couple standing at number 63.

Coroner – "What height was he?"

Evidential Details

<u>William Marshall</u> – *"About 5 ft 6 in., and he was rather stout. He was decently dressed, and I should say he worked at some light business* [barber], *and had more the appearance of a clerk than anything else.*

<u>Coroner</u> – "Are you quite sure this is the woman?

<u>William Marshall</u> – *"Yes, I am. I was standing at my door, and what attracted my attention first was her standing there some time, and he was kissing her. I heard the man say... 'You would say anything but your prayers'. They went down the street."*[civ]

Put off by what she knew, Liz laughed politely. She does not want to offend this powerful broad shouldered man. Her behavior seems to indicate she knew Jack and that he was trouble. As she walked along, she could have asked him not to bother her as this is an evening of opportunity realizing the weather for sex will be cooler after September.

The man went back into the Men's Educational Club, got another drink, and listened to the fiery speech about world revolution. Shortly after the members started to leave. "Around midnight...various people including a policeman saw her [Liz] chatting up a man or a succession of men."[cv]

As he drank and listened, Jack became aggravated by the idea of Liz putting him off while still soliciting. Isn't he good enough? Indifferent to the rhetoric, he left the club at around 12:30 a.m. and found her still at the Dutfield Yard entrance. Seeing him as an unwanted prospecting interruption, Liz moved across the street.

Police Constable William Smith, 26, (Badge 452H) saw a broad shouldered man (Jack) with Liz, between 12:30 – 12:35 a.m. while walking his beat. In a statement preserved by the British Home Office, Smith stated the suspect had a dark complexion, was about 5' 7" tall, [and] had a trimmed moustache. He was wearing a black 'diagonal' coat, hard felt hat, white collar and tie.[cvi]

<u>Coroner</u> – "Can you form any idea as to his age?

<u>P.C. Smith</u> – *"About **28** years.*

<u>Foreman</u> – "Was the man or the woman acting in a suspicious manner?

<u>P.C. Smith</u> – *"No.*[cvii]

Liz is aware the Marxists can be vehement and is cautious about causing a commotion. But this broad shouldered man will not take no for an answer. Shortly after 12:30 a.m. Liz moved around the corner east on Fairclough Street in an attempt to put some distance between herself and the IWEC while dealing with Aaron again. The man put his hand to the wall blocking Liz's forward movement while he spoke to her. Orator Morris Eagle returned to the IWEC at 12:35 a.m. while the confrontation on Fairclough was taking place.

At this time, Mr. James Brown, of 35 Fairclough Street, passed by.

At 12:45 he saw a woman with her back to the wall talking to a man (Jack) obstructing her passage.

<u>James Brown</u> – *"As I was going across the road I saw a man and woman standing by the Board School in Fairclough-street. They were standing against the wall. As I passed by them I heard the woman say, 'No, not tonight, some other night.' That made me turn around, and I looked at them. The man had his arm up against the wall, and the woman had her back to the wall facing him. The place where they were standing was rather dark. I should say the man was about 5 ft. 7 in. in height. He appeared to be a stoutish build.*

Rather than telling Aaron to get lost, Liz politely tells this customer *"not tonight."* With 80% of the Marxists having departed, this refusal is telling. This is his second rejection by a hooker approximately his mother's age. Liz is in danger, but Kosminski walked off in a huff up Berner Street toward Commercial Road.

As he walks he becomes more aggravated. Liz has rejected him twice. Tramping on, this gnaws on his drunken pride. The reason he hates women is because he has never been successful and as he marches his resentment builds. Abruptly he turned around before getting to Commercial Road. He will teach this whore a lesson. He will have his way and he is not going to pay. And if she gives him any trouble he has a knife.

Just as he turned back, Hungarian immigrant Israel Schwartz of 22 Helen Street, Back Church Lane, rounded the corner from Commercial Road onto Berner Street. He found himself some distance behind an intoxicated, broad shouldered man headed toward the IWEC alleyway. In a statement to police Schwartz described Jack, "...*age, about 30; ht, 5ft. 5 in.; comp., fair; hair dark; small brown moustache, full face, broad shoulders; dress, dark jacket and trousers, black cap with peak, and nothing in* (at) *Berner and Fairclough Streets intersection* (no second man) - *dimly lit on a misty London night in September, 1888."*

The Berner Street picture (right) was taken 21 years later (1909). On the corner was the Lord Nelson's PUB owned by Louis Hagens. The first door to the right is the residence of fruitier Matthew Packer and the second door was a 'tenement'. Liz scuffled with Aaron below the wagon wheel.

The three-story IWEC building should have been preserved as a museum to the origins of Communism. In 1903 Leon Trotsky and Vladimir Lenin visited. In 1907 Lenin and Joseph Stalin attended the Fifth Congress of the Russian Social Democratic Labor Party in Whitechapel. That assembly consolidated Lenin's Bolshevik leadership and discussed strategies for the Russian revolution that came in 1917. Those conferences included Communists Maxim Gorky and Rosa Luxembourg.

Evidential Details

The corner of Berner and Fairclough streets. A Swedish immigrant walked into a pitch black alley with a Polish immigrant below the wagon wheel entrance. Demolished by 1950, the three story building behind the wheel was Communism's cradle. After the Russian Revolution (1917), and once into Asia, that struggle went on to execute and uproot untold tens of millions of innocent people forcing them to live under totalitarian state control during the ill-fated 20th Century.

Evidential Details

By now Liz had moved back to the Dutfield Yard entrance to see what business remained. Schwartz then witnessed Kosminski walk up to her and start talking. The man grabbed Liz's shoulders and pushed her into the Dutfield alley. Jack means business and Liz should have protested loudly. But instead she resisted being taken into the alley and a scuffle broke out.

At this point the non-English speaking Schwartz, moved to the other side of the street as there was no one with a knife to worry about. He watched across and saw the stout man turn Liz around and throw her down on the sidewalk. She screamed three times but not very loudly, suggesting she was not really trying to summon help.[cviii] But this does account for the bruises in the medical report. "*Over both shoulders, especially the right, and under the collar bone and in front of the chest there was a blueish* (sic) *discoloration...*"

Questions remain as to why Liz didn't scream loudly or try to get help. But, it would have brought club members out into the street and she did not want that to happen. There is reason for this.

Mary Malcolm – "*I could not say where she was living except that it was somewhere in the neighbourhood of the tailors and Jews at the East-end.*[cix]
Elizabeth Tanner – "*She told me she worked among the Jews, and was living with a man on Fashion-street.*[cx]
Michael Kidney – "*She could also speak Yeddish.*[cxi] [Yiddish]

Elizabeth was now compromised. It was becoming clear Jack will ruin her efforts to capitalize on what is left of this gathering. So she was trying to draw his cooperation. The Jews offered cleaning and sewing jobs and the last thing she needed was to have everyone at the club know she was refusing to have sex with Aaron. He might tell his friends she had rejected him when everyone had seen her soliciting. She would have been concerned word of mouth could go out not to employ her. Sex with the Ripper had become political.

Liz's options were limited. It's almost 1:00 a.m. She's a pro. She can handle it. She needs the money and the good will. Faced with history's most deranged woman loathing serial killer, in an armed state of drunken aggravation, Liz puts a mint into her mouth and starts into the pitch black to perform any sex act he demands.

Exactly what happened in the alley for how long? After a detailed analysis Ripperologists agree, "*We just do not know enough to resolve these riddles.*"[cxii] And unknown to history, her move into the alley would reveal secrets greater than when she was exposed as a prostitute in Sweden.

McMoneagle – Into the alley - I think they found the tunnel [alley]**, which was really dark, and the woman tried to encourage the man into a sexual act for which she demanded payment. I believe he refused to pay her, and began to become rough with her. She struggled back,**

which only encouraged him as he was more excited by that, than the thought of sex.

Contemporary artist's interpretation of Liz going through the IWEC alley gates with Aaron Kosminski captioned "Going to her doom."

I believe this rage was brought on by this woman's struggles and he then began to strike her. She attempted to turn and run, but he grabbed her from behind in a sort of wrist lock around the throat and then killed her, by stabbing her in the neck from behind. Killer was right handed. He carried the knife in his right coat pocket. I get a sense that he was kind of wild about it and probably stabbed her at least three times, strangling her all the while with his arm to prevent her from crying out. When she ceased to struggle, he dumped her to the ground. He was drunk and very excited by it all...could also be some form of conflict between [the] killer and those he was trying to purge by killing.

In the case of man or woman, you have about twenty seconds MAX until you lose consciousness when the throat is cut. It has more to do with loss of blood to the brain than lack of oxygen to the blood. Usually, when someone's throat is cut, there is a loud exhalation of air, sort of sounds like the air rushing from a slashed tire. This is followed by a low gurgling sound which is the person choking on their own blood which fills the throat area, and then they lose consciousness.

Most military's do not cut the throat if they want to kill silently -- they throttle the throat with an arm lock and drive the point of the blade into the kidney area just below the rib cage. A) It's a much easier target; B) A much softer target; C) It causes immediate seizure, which prevents the person from either exhaling or inhaling/talking/yelling/or most anything else. Much quieter than getting one's throat cut. Death is usually very painful and takes about four minutes.[17]

---

[17] Mr. McMoneagle holds Army license certifications in knife fighting and bayonet.

Military Intelligence level likeness of Liz (45) the veteran. This picture shows her as she assessed the situation with Jack a couple of minutes before walking into the alley. With no takers at about 1:00 am, she still showed hesitation about a burley, strong armed man with a bad reputation whose belligerent propositions continued to focus on her.

JACK THE RIPPER

McMoneagle's Aaron Kosminski. This is the world's only portrait of "Jack". Unfortunately, as this was brought forward, there were no contemporary pictures available for comparison. Those images are still stowed away in Scotland Yard's archives under Victorian State secrecy directives.

McMoneagle – Elizabeth's final thoughts - My sense is that her thoughts are very confused - probably a result of alcohol and dying violently. I don't think she knew (he was the Ripper). **I think she thought this guy was killing her because she wouldn't put out or something.**

The corner of Berner and Fairclough streets. This 1873 map shows the Dutfield Yard behind the IWEC building with the alley alongside. Stride was knifed at the tip of the arrow. Kosminski ran behind the building and observed Diemshutz discover her.

With the drawings we asked McMoneagle if Liz knew Kosminski.

McMoneagle - I get a mixed reaction to this question. I get a sense of yes, but not that night. So, she may have gotten drunk with her killer on some other night and knew him.

Police surgeon Dr. George Bagster Phillips [1834-1897] later test-ified Liz's injuries could have been inflicted in a matter of a couple of seconds. Liz grabbed her throat as her right hand was bloodied. There was a division of her windpipe. She fainted, was thrown to the ground and bled out unmolested. The left carotid artery had been severed which pumped blood into the alley. It was just after 1:00 am.

McMoneagle – Dress - He was dressed in dark clothing, with a heavy black coat that appears to be split up the back to the waist. I believe his coat was longer than shorter; but still not full length. I believe he also had a preference for wearing a hat. He was wearing a hat that looks something like a derby.

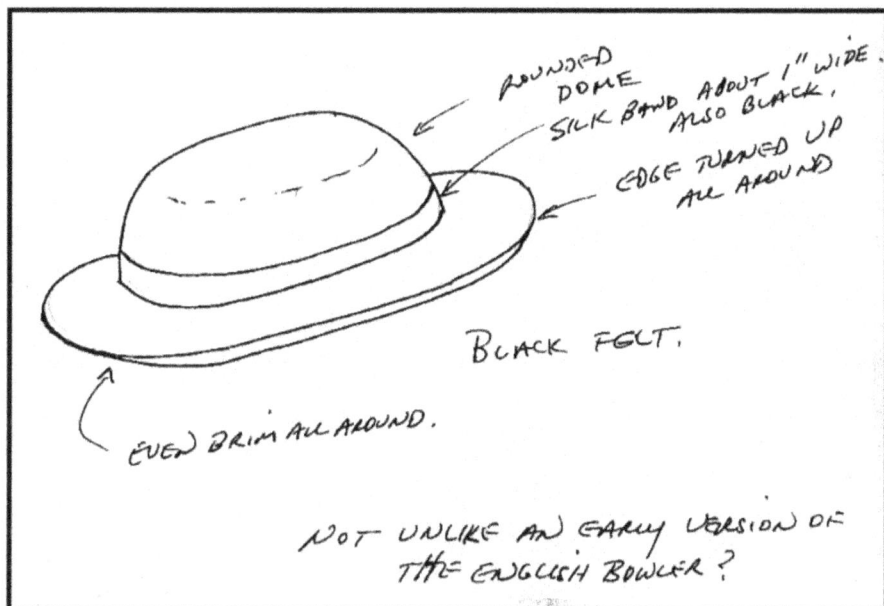

ROUNDED DOME
SILK BAND ABOUT 1" WIDE. ALSO BLACK.
EDGE TURNED UP ALL AROUND
BLACK FELT.
EVEN BRIM ALL AROUND.
NOT UNLIKE AN EARLY VERSION OF THE ENGLISH BOWLER?

Jack's disputed hat. The description says: "Rounded Dome. Silk band about 1" wide, also black. Edge turned up all around. Black felt. Even brim all around. Not unlike an early version of the English Bowler?" It did not have detective's flaps or a flat top.

Believe that he probably had committed murder before, but not necessarily women. If the records were checked, I believe you would find that there were similar murders of men within the same areas of the city about the same time. Probably murders put down to mugging. I think this guy had murdered before, but had murdered both women and men for money, or sex.

I think the hooker was simply a random target who looked something like his mother/ex, and was able to generate the buried rage he was hiding. His rage is normally under control, except for when he is drinking. I believe he normally does not go near women when he is drinking, as he knows they will only make him mad. But, on this particular night, this particular woman was trying to make some extra cash by getting it on with anyone she could meet at the local pub [IWEC]. I believe that this man probably would have had sex with her and then left her alive, if she had given it up instead of demanding money.

McMoneagle - The man who did the murder appears to be approximately five feet, six inches in height; heavy set and very brutish, maybe 180 to 200 pounds. Like a dockworker. Has a small well trimmed moustache, and is approximately 32-35 years of age. Slightly receding hairline, heavy side burns, full face.

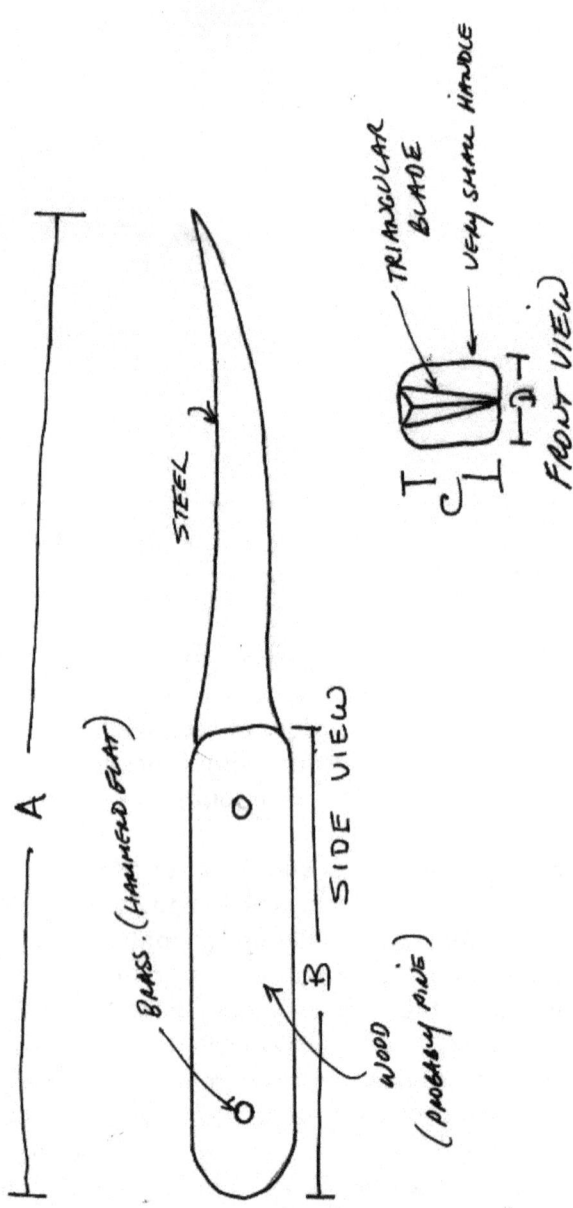

VERY MUCH LIKE A "FISH" KNIFE
PROBABLY USED FOR CUTTING BAIT
VERSUS FILETING.

TRIANGULAR BLADE

VERY SMALL HANDLE

FRONT VIEW

STEEL

BRASS. (HAMMERED FLAT)

WOOD (PROBABLY PINS)

A

B

SIDE VIEW

SCALE: APPROX. 2/3 RDS FULL SIZE.

ACTUAL SIZE = A: 10 INCHES; B: 5½ INCHES; C: 1⅛ INCHES; D: 1 INCH.

Jack's unknown knife. This drawing shows the draftsman level of detail military remote viewers offer U.S. Intelligence services. The top right text reads: "**Very much like a fish knife – Probably used for cutting bait versus filleting.**"

Jack was now in an alley, with a dying woman on the ground, as IWEC live-in steward Louis Diemshutz drove in. A jewelry dealer, he was returning from work at the Westow Hill Market, Crystal Palace, Sydenham. He noticed the time at 1:00 a.m. at a tobacco shop along the way. He swung his horse into the Dutfield Yard alley just as Liz was thrown to the brick. Aaron ran back to hide behind the building.

McMoneagle - Diemshutz arrival - Clicking sounds, like someone wearing heavy metal taps on the heels of their boots (hobnail boots) [horse hooves]. Get a sense this man "Louis Diemshutz" is moving slowly or carefully forward[18] – feeling his way with his hands, careful of where he is walking -- primarily because it is so dark. He can't see. He is leading a horse without a saddle. I believe Louis is trying to put his horse away inside the stable, but is having difficulty seeing where he is going.

He [Diemshutz] had to grope to find the body. Body was probably about twenty feet down inside the alleyway[19] (two thirds of the way to what feels like an enclosed courtyard or open area with a partially open roof to the sky. I believe that Louis arrived very soon after the murder and the man (Kosminski) might have still been somewhere close by, perhaps in a darkened alley. I get a strong sense that he watched Louis enter the tunnel... he was somewhere to the front and left of where the body was being discovered. Deep in shadows...

Diemshutz: *"My pony is rather shy and as I turned into the yard it struck me that he bore too much towards the left hand side against the wall. I bent my head to see what it was shying at, and I noticed that the ground was not level. I saw a little heap which I thought might be some mud. I touched the heap with my whip handle, and then I found that it was not mud. I jumped off the trap and struck a match. When I saw it was the body of a woman I ran indoors."*[cxiii]

McMoneagle - I get a sense that Louis is bending down and groping at something he has stumbled over. Get a distinct sense of blood and human waste. Probably a body or someone who has died. [It]...also smells heavily of booze and has rancid breath, not very hygienic. I think this frightens the heck out of Louis and he leaves his horse to run for help. He stumbles and falls while running away in the dark. But, returns later with people and lights, lanterns.

Louis went in to the club to get a lantern. Diemshutz and tailor machinist Isaacs Kozebrodsky went back into the alley and "struck a light"

---

[18] McMoneagle knows his name because I named him during the feedback session.
[19] According to the Police Report, the distance from her feet to the street was 12 feet placing her head 17.5 feet in from the street. The doctor's report said three yards to the street.

with Mrs. Diemshutz watching from the kitchen door. When she saw the body, she screamed alarming other club members. Jack the Ripper had struck again – right outside her kitchen door.

Louis Diemshutz was a Russian immigrant and the club steward who discovered Elizabeth's body.

THE FIFTH VICTIM OF THE WHITECHAPEL FIEND.

London Police Gazette

Police artist depiction of Diemshutz discovering the body showing similar north wall detail with Liz positioned on her back rather than on her side facing the wall. The cart pictured is known as a costermonger's barrow (right edge).

Two contemporary drawings of Diemshutz discovering Elizabeth. Her true body positioning is shown at top

When the men streamed into the alley, they found Elizabeth lying on her side along the wall. "Her left arm was extended and there was a packet of cachous - a pill used by smokers to sweeten the breath - in her hand. Her right wrist and hand were covered in blood. The legs were drawn up, with the feet close to the wall. There was mud on the left side of the face and her hair was matted on that side.

Mrs. Mortimer, living four doors away at 36 Berner Street, said: *"The body was lying slightly on one side, with the legs a little drawn up as if in pain, the clothes being slightly disarranged, so that the legs were partly visible."*[cxiv]

Police Constables Edward Collins [Badge 12 HR] and Henry Lamb, 37, [Badge 252H] would be the first police on the scene. The other officer was sent to find a doctor, while Morris Eagle went to Leman Street Police Station for assistance. Constable Lamb closed the wooden gates to the alley and waited for the Doctors to arrive. Inspector Charles Pinhorn, 39, and Chief Inspector West arrived at 1:25 a.m. Inspector Reid and Superintendent Arnold followed. Pinhorn would ultimately assume responsibility for the on-site investigation.

Police artist representation of Doctors Phillips and Kaye looking at
Elizabeth. The body is incorrectly shown with the head toward the street.

**McMoneagle - There is a body and the body is important for
some reason. Not what I would call attractive. I may be wrong about
this, however, as I am also getting a sense that she is an important
personage for some reason or another.**

**Believe most of what I described probably took place in a
maximum of ten minutes time. Also, believe it was so compressed in
time that by the time they got light to the alleyway or tunnel, the
woman's body was still basically warm to the touch.**

PC Henry Lamb - *"There was no one within a yard of it. As I was examining
the body some crowded round. I begged them to keep back, and told them
they might get some blood on their clothing, and by that means get themselves into trouble* [cxv]

Doctor Frederick William Blackwell, of 100 Commercial Road, was summoned by his assistant Edward Johnston to come to the crime scene.

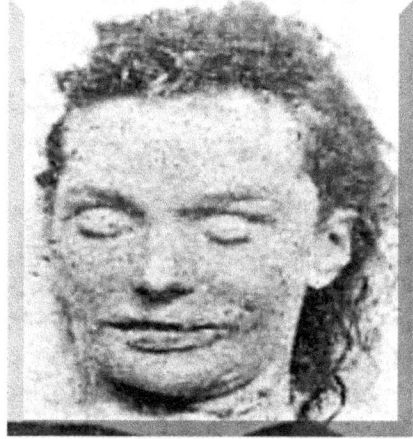

Johnston then went to the Dutfield yard with Constable Collins at approximately 1:05 a.m. when he briefly examined the body. Dr. Blackwell, 37, pronounced Elizabeth dead at 1:10 am. He later said, "The appearance of the face was quite placid."[cxvi]

Coroner – "How long had the deceased been dead when you saw her?

Dr. Blackwell – *"From 20 minutes to half an hour when I arrived. It was a very mild night and was not raining at* the time. Deceased could not have cried out after the injuries were inflicted as the windpipe was severed."[cxvii]

"Strides throat had been cut. The incision was 6 inches in length and commenced 2 1/2 inches in a straight line below the angle of the jaw; 3/4 of an inch deep over an undivided muscle, then becoming deeper. The cut was very clean and deviated downwards. The left carotid artery had been severed, from which death resulted."[cxviii]

Charles Letchford, living at 30, Berner Street, said: *I heard the commotion when the body was found, and heard the policemen's whistles, but did not take any notice of the matter, as disturbances are very frequent at the Club, and I thought it was only another row. The Club is occupied by what is known as the National Workmen's Educational Society, and is affiliated to the Socialist League, of which it is a foreign branch. Its members seem to be largely composed of Russian Jews, and Jews of other nationalities also find a welcome there. Berner-street is a very notorious part of Whitechapel. It is close to a district which was formerly known as Tigers Bay, because of the bad character of the persons who frequented it. A few yards distant is the house wherein Lipski murdered Miriam Angel.*[cxix]

McMoneagle – Ripper's mentality - I believe he was a little bit crazy and had a kind of rage against women inside of him. This rage was a result of having been badly treated by a woman he loved in his original home. It is sort of a mix of elicit sexual desire for his mother and [the] mother desire for a woman who wasn't his mother -- kind of a twisted want or desire neither woman wanted to give to him. [This] ...makes me think he probably hates women, especially women who remind him of his ex-lover and mother, as well as this hooker he killed.

Forty-five minutes after the murder and 20 to 30 after Dr. Blackwell arrived, Dr. George Bagster Phillips, 54, of 2 Spitalsquare, arrived to examine the crime scene. Twenty-eight on-lookers were detained for questioning. The body was removed to St George's Mortuary at 4:30 a.m. At 5:30 Constable Collins washed down the alley. When the news came out, a horrified public considered Liz to be the Ripper's fifth victim. And, as in all other Ripper murders, the authorities were baffled.

Subsequently, Mrs. Diemshutz told the press: "*Just about 1:00 a.m. Sunday I was in the kitchen on the ground floor of the club and close to the side entrance. I am positive I did not hear screams or sounds of any kind. Even the singing on the floor above would not have prevented me from hearing had there been any. In the yard itself all was as silent as the grave*"[cxx]

"After the body had been removed to St. George's Mortuary, the detectives entered the Club, and made a careful examination of the inmates. Their pockets were searched, their hands and clothing particularly scrutinized, and some of them allege that they were made to take off their boots. All knives had to be produced, and each man had to give an account of himself before he was allowed to depart. The police found nothing suspicious in the Club or upon its members, and in the late morning surveillance was withdrawn."[cxxi]

Dr. Phillips.
"HANG THE PAPERS"

At the autopsy, Dr. Blackwell cut while Dr. Phillips took notes. Later Phillips errored by ruling out intoxication, indicating there was no trace of malt liquor, anesthetic or narcotic in Liz's stomach. Yet, Elizabeth had been drinking and was known for frequent public drunkenness. The doctor had no basis to conclude she was not drinking at all. Her drink was a rum grog which explains why they could find no evidence of a malt beverage in her stomach.

In time statements were made by those attempting to reinvent the circumstances. Israel Schwartz was the only eyewitness and the police stated he had identified the killer at the police station. Aaron Kosminski should now be jailed and the murders stopped.

But later on Schwartz stated that he saw another man (Maybrick) on Berner Street who approached both Liz and Aaron! This second man story was a new addition to his police statement. What tips off the historian is that Schwartz initially said second man was holding a pipe. Then he told the papers the man was carrying a knife. It is doubtful such a crucial piece of information could have been confused or overlooked. From which door this man supposedly emerged was never mentioned. Moreover, if Maybrick was really holding a knife, Schwartz would definitely not have crossed the street to get within arm's length of him while watching Liz shuffle with Jack.

If Maybrick crossed the street to kill Stride, how did he simultaneously pursue Schwartz down the street at the same time Liz was knifed? And what was Kosminski doing the whole time? Watching? Nor were any of these people seen by Diemshutz as he came through the intersection on to the narrow Berner Street at 1:00 AM. Schwartz's timeline was not thought out and was clearly a bogus, last minute story for investigators.

Additionally, in the police statement the first man (Kosminski) tries to pull Stride from the passage! In the second, he tries to push her into the passage. In the Star interview, it is the second man (Maybrick) (not the first) who yells "a warning" as opposed to calling out "Lipski" as stated in the police statement. In the Star interview, the second man had a red moustache -- in the police statement, there is no mention of a moustache. The man is then described as having light brown hair when Aaron had black hair.

Schwartz knew the Ripper was stocky with broad shoulders. So his second man (Maybrick) was quite naturally tall and thin to deceive authorties. This provided the Maybrick Diary someone else to blame. Then on October 1, the *Star* newspaper reported an understatement from the Leman Street Police Station: *The truth of the man's* (Schwartz's) *statement is not wholly accepted."* The Ripper's only eyewitness was not even asked to testify at the inquest. With his evolving story it is time "Ripperologists" accept the second man was a complete fabrication to create more false light.

About his refusal to sign off on Jack, it is important for gentiles to understand there are very severe religious penalties for court testimony against a fellow Jew in a capital case. Israel Schwartz did not want to face this for simply walking home at the wrong time in a foreign country.

Jack fled when Diemshutz went into the club. Unbloodied he walked to the Great Synagogue on Duke Street universally referred to as St. James Place. He was now among friends that would not ID him. How long he loitered before his next victim happened along can only be estimate-ed. But just before the second murder in this "double event", Joseph Lawende, Joseph Hyam Levy and Harry Harris witnessed Kosminski talking to Catherine Eddows as she propositioned him. She was talking body to body close and putting her hand on his chest. They saw his face as her back was to them. But they all agreed they would not be able to recognize Jack again.

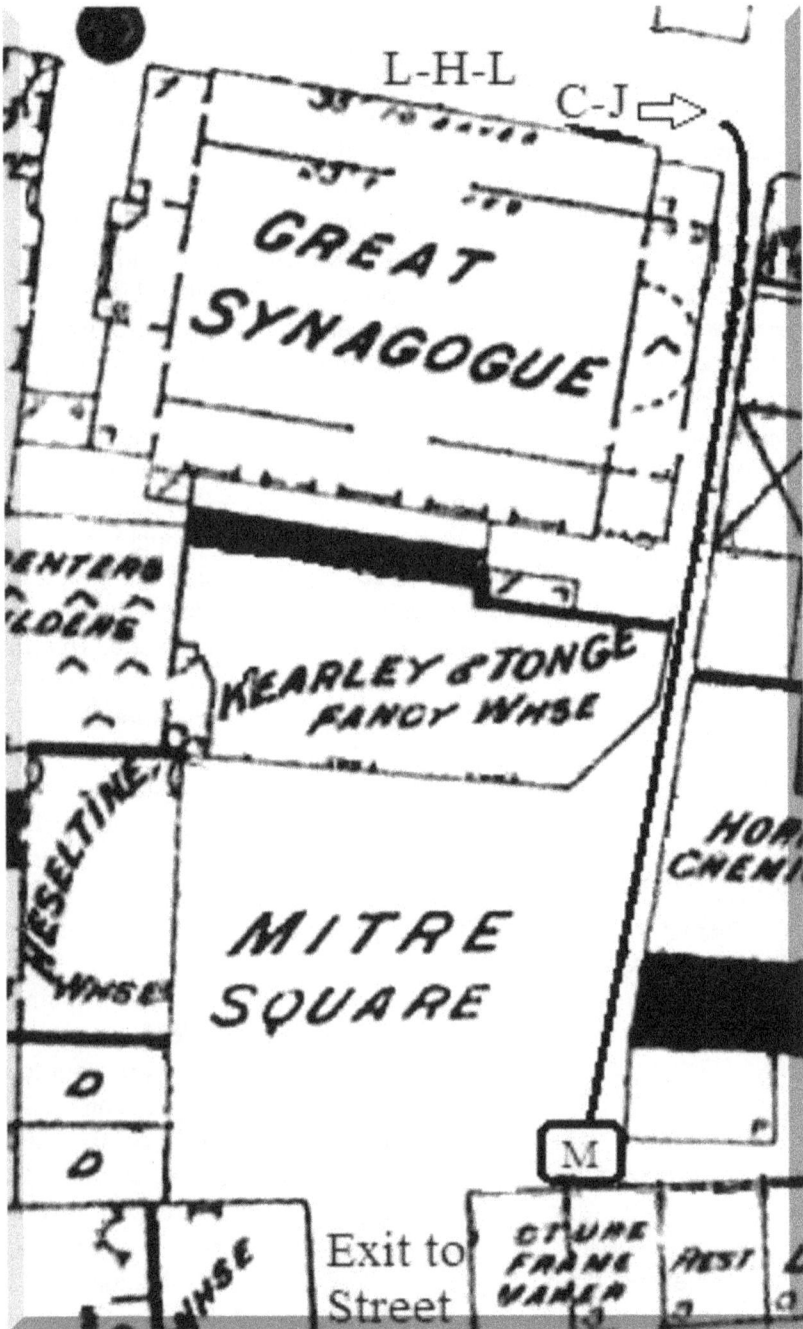

After killing Stride, Kosminski walked to the Great Synagogue on Duke Street [top] where he was seen talking to Lawende, Harris, Levy and later to Catherine Eddows (C-J top right). Agreeing to have sex, they went through the passageway [right side] to a corner in Mitre Square where the murder took place (lower right M).

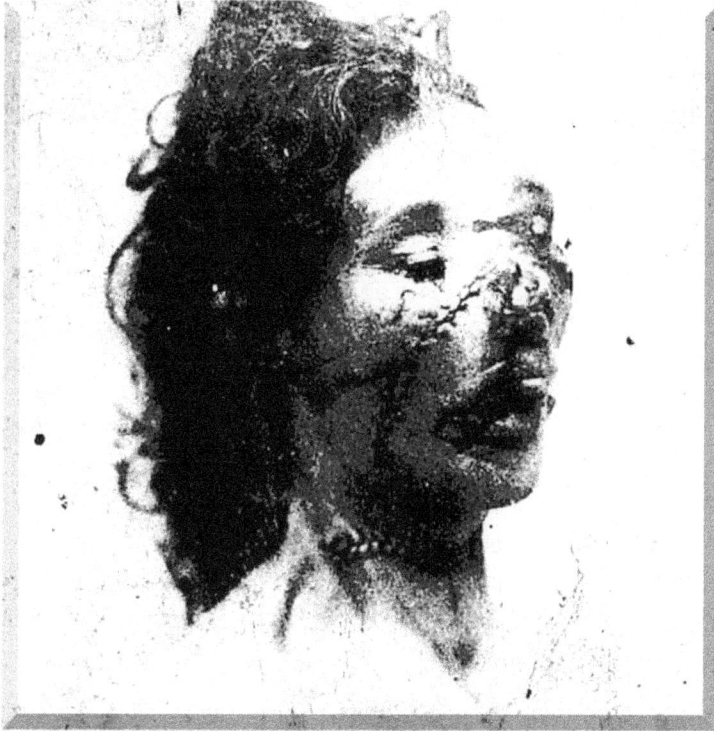

Catherine Eddows [1842 - 1888] – ripped approximately 45 minutes after Elizabeth Stride in the Ripper's legendary night of the "double event."

CID Eddows Diagram #2

The way Eddows body was discovered.

Lawende even falsified the color of his coat to "*salt and pepper*." After the Schwartz identification, the police knew who Jack was, but they could not charge him, as they had not caught him "red handed." And those that knew would not come forward because of the injustice to Israel Lipski.

Jack knew the area behind the synagogue. Catharine Eddows was taken through the passageway and ripped in the corner of Mitre Square behind the Duke Street Synagogue. What took place is Act II of the double event that brought London to a new panic level.

Eddows throat was slit. Her abdomen was opened from the groin to the breastbone. Her intestines were lifted up over her right shoulder. Her left kidney was removed along with most of the womb. Jack then lingered to mutilate her face. He pierced her eye, cut deep across her face, and cut off the tip of her nose. Her body was removed to the Golden Lane City Mortuary.

At 2:55 a.m., PC Alfred Long was walking his beat on Goulston Street. In the stairwell of the 108 - 119 Wentworth Model Dwellings, he spotted a piece of bloody apron whose material was subsequently matched to Eddows clothing. Aaron had momentarily ducked out of sight to clean up and scratch a message in his Polish English.

The cleaned Goulston Street stairwell wall.

Evidential Details

Above a bloody cloth was written on the wall: "*The Juwes are the men that will not be blamed for nothing.*" This message has been subject to varying interpretations – including outright denial - depending upon the author's religion. Based on the IWEC rhetoric, it was a statement that Jack disagreed with Marxism.

Police knowledge of the suspect's religion clears up questions about why the wall was immediately washed before press pictures could be taken. And now, with a gruesome ripping right in their backyard, the Rabbis Adler were pushed further in considerations of surrendering this profligate serial murderer to gentile justice. What should be done with this man who will probably rip again causing a wider uproar against the community? But to surrender Kosminski to a show trial and a hanging was out of the question. Could a deal be reached to get Aaron silently into an institution?

Eddowes had a funeral procession which attracted a crowd. Close to 1000 people attended a rally in Victoria Park demanding the resignation of the London Police Chief and the Home Secretary. The upshot from all the Ripper cover-up was that Kosminski was still on the street. The Rabbis likely had a word with him about what he was doing and how a massive backlash would hurt the community. If so, he was apparently indifferent. There is simply no time line here. But he did delay his next killing from September 30 to November 9.

On November 12, a George Hutchinson came to the police claiming he had been pan handled for six pence by Mary Jane Kelly the night of her murder. In his "Special Report", he said he had turned her away but then saw her walk up to Kosminski and they went over to Dorset Street together. As Kosminski passed by, he pulled his hat down over his eyes and Hutchinson grew suspicious.

Hutchinson: *I stooped down and looked him in the face. He looked at me stern.* That night he, *Wore a very thick gold chain. Respectable appearance. Walked very sharp. Jewish appearance. Can be identified.* cxxii

Aaron ripped Kelly inside her studio apartment to an unrecognizable level. Her gruesome autopsy is part of the historical record indicating a pathologist would need at least two hours to do an equivalent amount of damage to a corpse.

Mary Jane Kelly's death must have become the final straw for the Adlers. The Israelite community did not want a crime this hideous to reflect on them. From the day of his identification, the police had tailed Kosminski. But apparently their vigilance had tapered off as Jack also knew he had been identified and was now cat and mouse with the law.

With the Kelly crime the Queen got involved. Writing on November 10 to Prime Minister Salisbury:

With camera through the window, this is what landlord Thomas Bowyer saw when he looked to see if anyone was home in an effort to collect the November rent that Mary Jane Kelly was trying to earn. With entrails on the table (right side), in this original photo the wall behind her does not show the initials FM (Florie Maybrick) as was produced for the Maybrick Diary.

Victoria – *This new most ghastly murder shows the absolute necessity for some very decided action. You promised, when the first murder took place, to consult with you colleagues about it.*[cxxiii]

Salisbury had. He told the Queen an eyewitness had identified the killer but refused to swear him. The police wanted the Queen to know they were on top of things but that their hands were tied by the law. And it is at this point that all governmental documentary evidence comes to a halt.

McMoneagle – All participants in this target lived in the same general area or neighborhood. I get a sense the neighborhood's...in the center of a city.

* * *

Before 1900 only seven books were published about Jack the Ripper. By 1950, there were six more. By the 100th anniversary (1988) there were twenty-five more. And by 2008 there were ninety-eight more totaling 136; 72% written more than 100 years after the fact. The mystery was assisted by the Ripper suspects file being removed from the official records.

It was not until February, 1894 that the Criminal Investigations Division (CID) Chief, Sir Melville Leslie McNaughton [1853-1921] named the CID's three Ripper suspects. But his statements were not released until 1959. McNaughton wrote twice about Kosminski without naming him:

McNaughton: *"He had a great hatred of women, specifically of the prostitute class, & had strong homicidal tendencies; he was removed to a lunatic asylum about March of 1889. There were many circs* [circumstances] *connected with this man which made him a strong "suspect."*[cxxiv] And again:

McNaughton - *"He had a great hatred of women, with strong homicidal tendencies. He was (and I believe still is) detained in a lunatic asylum about March 1889. The man in appearance strongly resembled the individual seen by the City PC* [Police Constable] *near Mitre Square.*[cxxv] (Eddows death)

It is easy to conclude that once Queen Victoria was apprised of the entire situation, she thought of her beloved Benjamin Disraeli. Here was an opportunity to repay his devotion with devotion. She would protect his religious community from the massive backlash that appeared eminent.

No paperwork is available, but a deal was clearly worked out between the Jewish Members of Parliament, London's rabbinical community, Scotland Yard, the Special Prosecutors Office, and the Queen, through the Prince of Wales, to take Aaron Kosminski off the street. This, in return for guarantees of total secrecy that he not be tried or punished – just detained. The conundrum was that British law had to be circumvented. This man was to be imprisoned for life without the possibility of parole while being deprived of due process.

In order to achieve this, a massive cover-up with strict penalties was needed as by now there were many people involved. This seemed to be in each party's interest. It would protect the government from future defence demands to circumvent the criminal justice system. This special case must never be sited as precedent because the legitimacy of the entire British jurisprudence system could be put at risk in future capital prosecutions.

The masses were repelled by Marxist Theory and a crowd gathered outside the IWEC to protest. The double doors leading to the alley where Liz died [center left] were closed. After the Lipski demonstrations, this mob action convinced the Queen and the Rabbis that a cover-up was the only way to protect British women and the Jewish Community. A mystery was born.

An uneasy religious minority needed protection from public backlash. They wanted guarantees from the Monarch herself. But a 69 year old Queen, attended by nineteenth century medicine, could die anytime – certainly before the 40 years younger Aaron Kosminski. So to do the deal, the Rabbis Adler wanted guarantees from the future Monarch as well.

It is at this point attention is focused on the wayward, sexually conflicted, cross-dressing, Albert Victor Christian Edward - Prince Eddy, Duke of Clarence [1862-1892] and heir to the throne. Being the family's "black sheep", he was well positioned to play a clandestine representative/courier role into Whitechapel. But Prince Eddy had been caught-up in London's illegal homosexual underground, making him an undesirable for the honourable Chief Rabbi and his son to pursue this important mediation.

Rabbi Hermann Adler   Eddie – The Prince of Wales

It would be of interest to know what Nathan Adler thought of the Duke. The mandatory 70 year rabbinical retirement age had not yet been formalized. Nonetheless, the Rabbi had been in semi-retirement since 1879 and his son Hermann had been elected as the Rabbi in his own right. In order to turn a Jew over to gentile justice, on a capital crime, the leadership needed continued assurances of state sponsored secrecy. Knowing this side of town, Prince Eddy met with Hermann Adler to work out the details, with his father's oversight. Of course there is no documentation of this because both sides wanted it to remain permanently secret.

That a royal carriage was in Whitechapel is likely given the need for direct access to Victoria. Eddy could advise Her and various parties discreetly in person. As these men conferred, their final agreement was to continue in perpetuity. The discussions were along this line:
1) Religious authorities will surrender Aaron Kosminski into custody without legal charges;
2) Kosminski will be taken to an asylum to live out the rest of his natural life;
3) There will be no civil or criminal court action regarding this case;
4) A Parliamentary minute will bar anyone inside the government from

leaking information about this case for all time. Further, a confidential mem-
orandum will announce that anyone disclosing Jack's identity will face
irrevocable loss of pension, severe administrative discipline, and certain civil
liability for slander regarding something unprovable;

5) The Jewish Community will never acknowledge this exception to the rule
of law, as it must never be allowed to serve as precedent.

Victoria, Queen of England [1819-1901], granddaughter of King George III, who waged war against the American Revolution. She reigned 63 years and was the first monarch to be photographed. Her most significant impact on world history was to provide a cradle for Marxism when it had been expelled from Europe. This picture was taken three years before the Ripper murders.

Alexander Bassano - Royal Archives, Windsor

For reasons including Jack, Queen Victoria left instructions that the transcription of her personal diary be heavily edited after her death, and then burned. This began in 1901 by her youngest child Beatrice. The process of reading, transcribing snippets, and then burning her diaries took many years. "It can be stated that Princess Beatrice felt constrained not merely to destroy, without transcribing, substantial portions of her mother's diary, but also to alter substantially a great many other portions which she did transcribe and it must be added that posterity has suffered in consequence an incalculable and irreparable loss."[cxxvi]

On November 16, 1907 all of Victoria's "very private" correspondence with Disraeli, discovered in Lord Rothchild's possession, were ordered burned. This and Beatrice's burning, would forever cover-up the depth of her affection for Benjamin Disraeli. King Edward VII knew something about all this and his correspondence with Victoria was also burned. Thus the mystery was sustained at the highest levels.

As Regent of all her people, Queen Victoria saw the perfect opportunity to cherish Disraeli's memory. Even though the Police had failed to catch the Ripper red handed, they did have London's entire male population reduced down to three men when Schwartz observed Kosminski with Stride. For the public, the Ripper crimes had simply stopped, just as mysteriously as they had started. But in the bureaucracy, this matter was viewed differently. No mention was made public until Major Arthur Griffiths published a book ten years later called *Mysteries of Police and Crime.*

The Ripper affair left resentments in metropolitan law enforcement and at Scotland Yard. The police had to bear the indignation that they were utterly incompetent when actually the opposite was true. They were forced to perpetrate the myth against themselves that Jack had gotten away.

In 1910, Scotland Yard's Dr. Robert Anderson was the first to partially blow the whistle on the Ripper's identity attempting to give England's law enforce-ment professionals their due.

This resentment was apparent with the first leak. Upon retirement in 1901, the Assistant Commissioner in charge of the CID at Scotland Yard, Dr. Robert Anderson [1841-1918], said that the police had done a phenomenal job. Early on, the police had narrowed the Ripper down to M.J. Druitt; Aaron Kosminski, and a Russian named Michael Ostrog. During the time of the Kelly murder, suspect Michael Ostrog was convicted of theft on November 14, in Paris, France. He was committed to a "lunatic asylum" as a homicidal maniac who poisoned women. Stating his overseas whereabouts in France were never determined when Kelly was murdered is simply subterfuge. This narrowed the suspects list to two.

Montague John Druitt's [1857-1888] body was found on December, 31 in the Thames River eight weeks after the last murder. A med-school *dropout*, he sought to become a *lawyer*. He had no murderous tendencies, was never seen in the area of the murders, and was never a suspect. He had become distraught when he lost his job due to what he believed was creeping insanity inherited from his legally insane mother. He was never a credible suspect. Had he died 90 days earlier he would be unknown. Aaron Kosminski was seen on Berner Street in front of the Dutfield Yard alley and later in front of the passage leading to Mitre Square, and then with Mary Jane Kelly on Dorset Street the night she died.

Then, in a serialized crime reminiscence in *Blackwood's Magazine*, Part VI, published in March 1910, a disgusted Robert Anderson wrote about Jack saying:

"...that he was living in the immediate vicinity of the scenes of the murders; and that, if he [Ripper] was not living absolutely alone, his people knew of his guilt, and refused to give him up to justice. And the conclusion we came to was that his people were low-class Jews, for it is a remarkable fact that people of that class in the East End will not give up one of their numbers to Gentile justice. And the result proved that our diagnosis was right on every point. For I must say at once that "undiscovered murders" are rare in London, and the "Jack the Ripper" crimes are not within that category. In saying that he was a Polish Jew I am merely stating a definitely ascertained fact. Scotland Yard can boast that not even the subordinate officers of the department will tell tales out of school, and it would ill become me to violate the unwritten rule of the service. In a footnote he added:

"I will only add that when the individual whom we suspected was caged in an asylum, the only person who had ever had a good view of the murderer at once identified him, but when he learned that the suspect was a fellow-Jew he (Schwartz) declined to swear him."

Still chaffing, Anderson decided to play the political game. He would risk his pension for the men. He knew that for the government to take his retirement they would have to declare he had violated the directive not to reveal the murderer forcing them to confirm Jack's identity. But the state did not respond and he kept his pension as part of the cover-up.

Next, in 1912, a series of articles were written by Hargrave L. Adam called *"Scotland Yard and its Secrets"*. In it Adam wrote: *"Sir Robt Anderson has assured the writer that the assassin was well known to the police, but unfortunately, in the absence of sufficient legal evidence to justify an arrest, they were unable to take him."*[cxxvii] These statements were not ignored.

In the House of Commons, a Member of Parliament, Mr. Mac Veagh, asked the Home Office Secretary: *"whether he (Anderson) obtained the sanction of the Home Office or Scotland Yard authorities to [approve] such publication; and if not, whether any, and if so what, steps should be taken with regards to it."* To which Lord Randolph Henry Spencer Churchill [1849-1894], father of Winston Churchill replied:

Lord Churchill: *"Robert Anderson neither asked for nor received any sanction to the publication..."* To which Mr. Mac Veagh inquired as to whether there wasn't a Parliamentary minute expressly prohibiting the publication of such documents.[cxxviii]

Mr. Mac Veagh received no answer. No one had the authority to confirm such a prohibition. Jack was a state secret neither to be acknowledged or denied. But this demonstrated that the authorities did know, and that they had gone so far as to initiate a Parliamentary minute on behalf of the cover-up. It is clear Jack was never a real mystery.

The Criminal Investigations Division (CID). Given the scenario, these men were particularly aggrieved to know their lot was to go down in history as the most incompetent law men in British history. This was due to the bending of laws that had been written in stone for centuries

Next Swanson's grandson James, brought forward his copy of Robert Anderson's *The Lighter Side* book. In the margins, Swanson [1848-1924] had written on the page of his personal copy, "*because the suspect was also a Jew and also because his* [Schwartz's] *evidence would convict the suspect, and witness would be the means of the murderer being hanged, which he did not wish to be left on his mind.*" DSS

Inspector Swanson wrote further on the book's end paper, "*After the suspect had been identified at the Seaside Home where he had been sent by us with difficulty in order to subject him to identification and he knew he was identified.*

On suspect's return to his brother's house in Whitechapel he was watched by police (City CID) *by day and night. In a very short time the suspect with his hands tied behind his back...was sent to Stepney Work-house and then to Colney Hatch and <u>died shortly afterwards</u>* – Kosminski *was the suspect* – DSS. Indicating he died shortly afterwards is an error that mystery defenders use to throw out everything he ever said. Inspector

Frederick Abberline [1843-1929] became the go to man in the Maybrick Diary when he told the press:

Abberline: *"You can state most emphatically that Scotland Yard is really no wiser on the subject than it was fifteen years ago."* But this statement had a double meaning. The Yard had all they needed in 1888 and Abberline's pension was never threatened.

Abberline: *"It is simple nonsense to talk of the police having proof he is dead. I am, and always have been, in the closest touch with Scotland Yard and it would have been next to impossible for me not to have known about it. Besides, the authorities would have been only too glad to make an end out of such a mystery, if only for their own credit."*[cxxix] (Author's underlining)

Exactly. The statement provides insight to their views, and that Jack's date of death was knowable. This also explains why author Stephen Knight remarked: *"It is surprising that, after the wealth of written notes in the [Scotland] Yard files relating to [previous victims] Nichols and Chapman, those on the remaining Ripper victims are almost empty."*[cxxx]

With Kosminski's removal from the street, and the rabbinical under-standings, the paperwork was removed from the file. How else could his identity be protected and the Justice system's orderly functioning be upheld? This also explains why Abberline's diary entries are missing between October 1887 and March 1891. Were there other crimes by Kosminski, "**put down to mugging**" that McMoneagle mentioned? It is unclear if there was any financial motive as the economic viability of Jack's barber shop has never been determined.

Detective Abberline was the Unit's Inspector in charge and he never said a word about the Ripper. His diary pages 44 and 45 are available.

Abberline: *"I think it is just as well to record here the reason why as from the various cuttings from the newspapers as well as the other matters that I was called upon to investigate – that never became public property – it must be apparent that I could write many things that would be very interesting to read.*

At the time I retired from the service the authorities were very much opposed to retired officers writing anything for the press as previously some retired officers had from time to time been very indiscreet in what they had caused to be published and to my knowledge had been called upon to explain their conduct – and in fact – they had been threatened with actions for libel."[cxxxi] Writing in 1903, Abberline revealed what was happening inside:
1) the Chief Inspector of the Metropolitan Police Criminal Investigations Div.;
2) the CID's Chief Constable at Scotland Yard, and;
3) the senior Detective of the Metropolitan Police Force, all ether made reference to a Polish Jew - not by name - or played a shell game. No other insiders spoke publically or wrote about it.

Inspector
Abberline
(left)

(Right) Her Majesty's Royal Coroner for East Middlesex, Wynne Edwin Baxter [1844 - 1920]. With the cover-up, it is understandable why his Inquest papers are a missing public record. He left no diary or papers concerning his Ripper inquests.

Vestry-hall, Cable-street; St. George's-in-the-East, London. An artist's view of the Coroner's Inquest proceedings room as Diemshutz answers questions before the Board of Inquiry regarding the Stride murder.

At a fifth inquest on London's East End Coroner Wynne Edwin Baxter was a "flamboyant" dresser and combative personality. Having won a bitterly contested election in 1887, his insistence that Jack had anatomical knowledge diverted police resources and has mislead investigators and historians ever since.

Released into his brother's custody, the Colony Hatch Insane Asylum Admissions book shows Aaron Kosminski, from [his brother's] Sion Square address, was committed to the Asylum on Feb. 7, 1891. *"The lay witness, however, Jacob Cohen, was a fellow Jew with an interest in pre-serving his tribe's reputation, and his assertion that* (unliquored) *Kosminski was a harmless imbecile may be untrustworthy."*[cxxxii] From there Kosminski went to the Leavesden Asylum where he died in 1919 at age 54.

For whatever the negotiations between Rabbi Adler and the author-ities, it took until March, 1889 to get Kosminski off the street. Passive when not drinking, he was admitted to the Mile End Old Town Workhouse Infirmary for three days where he was verified insane for at least the past two years. Eventually Aaron Kosminski had to be restrained for "mild violence" against asylum staff when he was forced to bath.

* * *

The night of Elizabeth's death, Mary Malcolm went to bed at 50 Eagle Street, Red Lion Square, Holborn. The day had been...well...discon-certing. Mary Malcolm and her sister Elizabeth Watts [Liz] were accustomed to meeting Saturday afternoons for about an hour to maybe ninety minutes. These get-togethers were valued as an opportunity to catch up on one another's life as only sisters can. Plus, Liz could learn a little something from seamstress Mary as she was interested in improving her skills. Regarding the day of their scheduled meeting, Mary testified in the Coroner's Hearings: Mary Malcolm – *"Before that she had not missed a Saturday for between two and three years. She always came at 4 o'clock in the afternoon, and we used to meet at the corner of Chancery-lane. On Saturday afternoon I went there at half-past 3, and remained there until 5, but* [the] *deceased did not turn up.*[cxxxiii]

Mary did give Elizabeth some money to help out. But what troubled her was that her sister failed to mention not being able to make the appoint-ment the Thursday before. Pondering, Mary Malcolm fell asleep while over in Whitechapel Liz was approaching the IWEC building.

The severing of one carotid artery does not produce immediate death. After being knifed and thrown to the ground, a conscience Liz had time to think before passing away. Given her increasingly hopeless middle age situation, with nowhere to go but back to Kidney - she may have accept-ed death.

Elizabeth's energy departed her fleshy envelope sometime around 1:10 a.m. which resulted in the following sworn Inquest testimony:
Mary Malcolm – *"About 1:20 a.m. Sunday morning I was lying on my bed when I felt a kind of pressure on my breasts, and then I felt three kisses on*

my neck. I also heard the kisses, and they were quite distinct."[cxxxiv]

In what was an unsettling experience, Mary later claimed she questioned why this happened on the night her sister had failed to show up for their weekly rendezvous.

Mary Malcolm – "*On Sunday morning, when I read the paper* (double event news), *I wondered whether it was my sister. I had a presentiment that it was.*"

Dark forebodings so moved Mary that she went to the police station to view the corpse. She was conducted over to the St. George's-in-the-East Mortuary. Through the difficulties of wet matted hair and a death mask face in flickering gaslight, she said she did not recognize Elizabeth. But bothered, she returned the next day to view the body again. This time she confirmed Elizabeth as her sister due to having viewed a black mark on her leg from an adder snake bite. As children, Mary had been bitten on the finger by the same snake. Mary Malcolm then officially claimed Elizabeth Gustafsdotter Ericsson's body as her sister Elizabeth Watt's and started to grieve.

Reputed to be a picture of the Saint George's in the East Mortuary circa 1910. This was where the people came to view the body. It was Liz's last location before the grave.

Mary Malcolm – "*I have seen the body in the mortuary. I saw it on Sunday and twice yesterday. It is the body of my sister, Elizabeth Watts.*
Coroner – You have no doubt about that?
Mary Malcolm – "*Not the slightest.*
Coroner – "You had some doubts as first?
Mary Malcolm – "*I had, but not now.*[cxxxv]

And now from the testimony came one last historically over looked clue determining what had happened to a young farm girl in Sweden almost a quarter century earlier. This was human conduct much more captivating than serial murder. Behavior so unusual that the third largest American clinical management company's medical librarian could find no statistics or even a reference to its incidence.[20]

Elizabeth carried no ID. Making matters worse, people came forward that complicated identification. Liz was identified as Annie Fitzgerald. And a prostitute named "One Armed Liz" [Elizabeth Burns, 18] was accompanied by H Division Police Sergeant William Thick to the mortuary and identified Liz as Wally Warden. Another said Annie Morris. Liz may have used all these names, particularly as the name Annie came back twice.

She was positively identified at the Mortuary by John Arundell and Charles Preston. But her boyfriend Michael Kidney and step nephew in law Police Constable Walter Frederick Stride, 30, (Badge 62349) would be the ones to make the final identification. Constable Stride testified at the Inquest he recognized Elizabeth as the woman his Uncle John Stride married when he was 11 years old. Elizabeth certainly knew of him and did not want Stride's name to be connected to her, so these aliases made sense.

Regarding her murder, Chief Inspector Donald Sutherland Swanson wrote: "*It may be shortly stated that the inquiry into her history did not disclose the slightest pretext for a motive on behalf of friends or associates or anybody who had known her.*"[cxxxvi]

On October 1, 2, 3, 5, and 23, the Stride Inquest was convened - Coroner Baxter, 44, presiding. Mary Malcolm swore, under penalty of perjury, the deceased was her sister. Even after days of grieving she broke down at the Inquest while testifying. "One newspaper commented that she seemed "*deeply affected*" as she gave her evidence. Upon several occasions during the examination she burst into tears."[cxxxvii] Such was the love for her "blood kin" Elizabeth.

But the police were not happy with Mrs. Malcolm. They had seen Long Liz in and out of the system. Nonetheless, they discontinued their next of kin search pending Inquest results.

Mary Malcolm was one of four brothers and sisters whose maiden name was Perrin. She had grown up in Colerne, near Chippenham, Wilts.[cxxxviii] Through standard death notification Mary Malcolm's real sister – now divorced and remarried as Elizabeth Stokes of 5 Charles Street, Tottenham – was officially notified of her own death! She had not seen her sister Mary in about 15 years, and was, at that time, married to her first husband named Watts, a wine merchant.

---

[20] Psychological investigational work concluded in February 1998. This vast specialty medical library included expensive Internet subscription medical reference sites yielding nothing.

Evidential Details

During these days Mary Malcolm had been reminiscing her many close and even exasperating moments with Liz. Her psychological ties to her sister as among the living were by now dissolved. One can imagine the stupefaction Mary Malcolm experienced when she learned her real sister, under a new last name, was to appear at the next coroner's hearing.

A grief stricken Mary Malcolm's only released likeness. The drawing shows a question mark in front of the words "? Sister of the Victim" [top right] confirming contemporary questions surrounding her sworn testimony.

After days of melancholy, Mary's psychological collision with reality must have left her devastated and bewildered. Worse, she became a police target as authorities had to re-open their search for the corpse's true identity. Suspicious, police wanted to know why Mrs. Malcom had deliberately interfered in the investigation of London's worst serial killer. The police were at a loss for a motive as to why an unrelated and respectable middle aged lady would attempt to claim a hooker for a family member burial.

What Mary Malcolm suffered is the process known as "transference". "*Most generally, the passing on, displacing or 'transferring' of an emotion or effective attitude from one person onto another person or object.*"[cxxxix]

Mary Malcolm was happy to have her sister (Liz) back, while Elizabeth revealed her thoughts about losing her family in Sweden. Here was a chance at sisterly love. Mary emerged as the most significant relationship in Liz's life since her "family" was drown on the *Princess Alice* in 1878.

Liz was again living a dual life just as a young prostitute/nanny during the early 1860's in Goteborg. Older and wiser, she never told Mary where she lived taking care not to make mistakes that bedeviled her in Sweden. She had taken her double life facility to a new level. She successfully concealed background from Mary Malcom for half a decade. She had found true family acceptance except this time she was undone by Jack.

But put yourself in the position of making a weekly appointment, in another country to masquerade as a sibling to a foreign national in their language. The average adult would tire of interloping with a stranger for a little money. It is unlikely anyone would return for a whole year, much less five. After a while the average adult would feel contempt for any one deluded enough to acknowledge an immigrant as blood. This would surface inadvertently in an off handed remark or indifferent facial expression.

Beyond this, consider the challenges. Even if someone had nothing better to do than entering into the weekly process of becoming a stranger's kin, each new meeting was a performance to avoid a very interpersonal unmasking. Imagine discussing dozens of childhood remembrances like a mutual snake bite, a bad foot, a common mother, the same childhood household, schools and the characterization of relatives you never met. Then you have to remember what had been said previously.

Conversations about churches, husbands, adolescent strife, childhood dolls, parties, and a host of events, the kids, inferences and nuances so pervasive they can never be adequately summed up. Although she met Mary's husband once, Liz also had to adroitly dodge yearly holidays, family reunions, other siblings, family friends and bygone acquaintances. This performance betrays a desire for family approaching obsession.

Sigmund Freud: "*The obsessive act serves to express unconscious motives and ideas. Obsessions are always reproaches reemerging in a transmuted form.*"[cxl]

Elizabeth's behavior was a clear cry for family attachment manifesting itself in sociologically undocumented behavior. But what really sets this apart is that Liz successfully overcame the disability that English was her second language. Psychologists consider this as among the most difficult of games to play - this being perhaps the only documented case in world history of successfully prolonged foreign language sibling impostering.

Properly written, Liz's sister acts could be the backdrop for a Shakespearian tragi-comedy where each time these women met, the aware audience would be held fast. But this sisterhood provided endearing feelings for both women. "Mrs. Malcolm seemed to bear a physical resemblance to Long Liz and clearly knew things that others corroborated."[cxli] Boyfriend Kidney stated Mrs. Malcolm looked like Liz.

The chest pressure and nocturnal kisses in Mary Malcolm's sworn testimony are what put her in motion to the police. Elizabeth had let her real sister down decades ago. Therefore, this was so important that after death she was able to find a way to encroach on three dimensions to tell her surrogate sister how deeply she cared. And to give a signal, perhaps, that she was aware she had now let Mary down as well. In Elizabeth's world the idea of letting another loved one down was sensitive and emotional. So, we asked McMoneagle:

Question: "Does a dead person have the ability to affect matter within the confines of three dimensions?"

McMoneagle - Probably they have more ability than even they know or understand about. I suspect however, that the focus is so much on the dying process or what is happening and where they are heading, that very little is done within the "here." Other than maybe a short mental message to <u>very close loved ones</u>, "Hey I've just died. Don't worry about me." That sort of thing.

As far as post death (say a few weeks or years down the pike after death), forget it. The personality of the person has made such drastic changes in state, and has refocused on issues we wouldn't even understand, they probably have no interest in "here" any longer.

Liz had learned her lesson and had been savvy. Mary Malcolm denied she was from Sweden, said she never heard the name Stride, said Liz was married to a large wine and spirits dealer and thought she was 37 years old. She had gone to view the body of her "sister" many times.

The reason Mary Malcolm had invested so much into her relationship with Liz soon became apparent. She had to put up with the negativism of her real sister again. Apparently not having been advised on the fact Mary Malcolm's October 2nd Inquest testimony referred to Liz's life, Mrs. Stokes started in on her sister.

<u>Elizabeth Stokes</u> "*Mrs. Malcolm, who gave evidence at the inquest, is my sister, but I have not seen her for years, and I do not expect to see her until I attend the adjourned inquest on the 23rd inst. My sister, Mary Malcolm, has never, as she swore, given me any money. It is untrue that I saw her on the Thursday preceding the murder. I never used to meet her, as she said, in Red Lion Street, to receive 1s* (shilling) *from her. I am not short of clothes, and I never lived in Commercial road nor kept a coffee house in Poplar. I may take a little drink now and then, but my sister never saw me in drink.*[cxlii]

Again, "On 23 October she (Elizabeth Stokes) inveighed bitterly against Mary Malcolm at the inquest. "*Her evidence was infamy and lies'* she cried heatedly, *'and I am sorry that I have a sister who can tell such dreadful falsehoods.*""[cxliii] As the ordeal unraveled, Mary Malcolm failed to appear.

Even with this sworn Inquest testimony "Ripperologists" have callously portrayed Elizabeth as a "*habitual self-dramatizing liar*"[cxliv] and that hers was merely a "*fanciful tale*", or a "*hooker masquerade.*" Focusing on the details of Jack's crimes, these writers have failed to see what may be the Ripper saga's most significant event. It is certainly a poignant insight into what happened to one of his victims as a young Swedish woman.

Elizabeth was part of a sequence of throat slittings and disembowelings of mostly middle aged women, killed without provocation, by an assassin that escaped into the night in the fall of 1888. And so now it was time. Liz was buried in the East London Paupers Cemetery, square 37, plot#

15509 on Saturday, October 6, 1888. The Swedish church paid G.C. Hawkes, of 41 Banner Street, for her undertaking.

Elizabeth was a long way from her prosperous Swedish homestead west of Gotebørg, Sweden. Gustaf and Beata Ericsson's little girl was gone. On her day there was no attempt to repatriate the body, no headstone for well over a century, no coffin, no ceremony, no clergy, nobody. Just a quiet grave digger labouring over what Shakespeare referred to as the, *rotten mouth of death*. It is unknown when her wistfully remembered family learned their relative was lost to the "double event" of the most noteworthy crime spree in British history.

She cannot be contacted, indicating she will only communicate with members of her family. Nonetheless, she has come to life again through seven different actresses in as many movies. Jack lived on another 31 years.

Elizabeth Stride's death certificate

Shadowy deeds to brick dust borne,
T'was bent with coat pocket thrust,
Plain sight hidden with drunken soul blackthorn,
Whose nether corpse blood ever did encrust.

~ Author ~

Lizabeth Gustafsdotter Ericsson Stride. With the mud washed out of her hair and no identification, she was cleaned, covered with a black throw and prepared for visitors. The knife wound can be seen on her neck (left). Her mouth wound can be seen +10 years later. Though other mortuary photos likely exist, this is the only picture released to the public.

A "grace marker" was erected in the 21st century.
She is the only Ripper victim to have a curb surround grave.

Fear no more the frown o' the great,
Thou art passed the tyrant's stroke;
Care no more to clothe and eat,
To thee the reed is as the oak.

Shakespeare – *Cymbeline*

Bibliography

- Begg, Paul,
    - *Jack the Ripper - The Uncensored Facts*; Robson Books; 1988
    - *Jack the Ripper A-Z*; Paul Begg, Martin Fido and Keith Skinner; Headline Book Publishing PLC, 1996
- Centralen; *The History of Goteborg*; Goteborg tourist information web site, 1997
- Davis, Lee, *Man-Made Catastrophes*; Facts on File, Inc. 1993
- Edited by Fodor, Nandor and Gaynor, Frank, *Freud - Dictionary of Psychoanalysis*; Fawcett Premier Publications; 1958
- Fido, Martin, *The Crimes, Detection and Death of Jack the Ripper*; Barnes & Noble, 1993
- Harrison, Shirley, *The Diary of Jack the Ripper*; Hyperion, 1993
- *History of the Central Synagogue series*, Pre 1900, 1900 – 1945, 1945 – 1970
- Jakubowski Maxim and Braund, Nathan, *The Mammoth Book of Jack the Ripper*; Robinson Publishers, 1999
- Kamenka, Eugene; *The Portable Karl Marx*; Penguin Books, 1983
- Knight, Stephen *Jack the Ripper: The Final Solution*; Academy of Chicago Publishers, 1986
- Nash, Jay Robert, *Darkest Hours*; A Wallace Book published by Pocket Books; 1976
- Reber, Arthur, *Dictionary of Psychology*; Penguin Books USA, Inc. 1995
- *Records of the Coroners Inquiry*; South-Eastern Division of Middlesex; Vestry Hall, Cable Street, St. George's-in-the-East, London, England
- *Report of the Director of the Public Prosecutions'*, (Public Accounts Committee), Parliamentary Papers (1899)-
- *Report of Chief Inspector Swanson*, Home Office records 144/221/A49301C/8a, Oct. 19, 1888, Thames Magistrates' Court, Court Register – 1887
- Sugden, Philip, *Complete History of Jack the Ripper*; Constable & Robinson, 1994
- Thomas, Donald, *The Victorian Underground* by; New York University Press, 1998
- Tully, James, *Prisoner 1167 - The Madman Who Was Jack the Ripper*; Carroll & Graf Publishers, Inc.; 1997
- Weintraub, Stanley, *Victoria, An Intimate Biography*; Truman Talley Books/E.P. Dutton New York 1987
- Woodham-Smith, Cecil, *Queen Victoria*; Dell Publishing Company, 1972
- Yost, David, *Elizabeth Stride and Jack the Ripper – The Life and Death of the Reputed Third Victim*; MacFarland & Company, Inc. Publishers 2008

Princess Diana

[i] McMoneagle, Joseph W., *Remote Viewing Secrets – A Handbook*; Hampton Roads Publishing Company, Inc. 2000 p. xv
[ii] McMoneagle, Joseph W., *The Stargate Chronicles*; Hampton Roads Publishing Company, Inc. 2002 p. 182
[iii] Simmons, Simone, *Diana – The Secret Years* with Susan Hill; Ballantine Books 1998 p.120
[iv] Delorm, Rene, *Diana & Dodi - A Love Story - By the Butler Who Saw Their Romance Blossom*, with Barry Fox and Nadine Taylor; Tallfellow Press 1998 p.144
[v] Anderson, Christopher, *The Day Diana Died;* William Morrow and Company 1998 p.114
[vi] Anderson; p.113
[vii] Delorm; p.154
[viii] ibid; p.154
[ix] The Learning Channel Presentation - *Princess Diana*; A Fulcrum Production; a Granada Presentation for ITV 1998; hereafter referred to as *TLC*
[x] Delorm; p.155
[xi] Anderson; p.99
[xii] ibid; p.166
[xiii] Sancton, Thomas and Scott MacLeod, *Death of a Princess - The Investigation*; St. Martin's Press 1998 p.157
[xiv] Delorm; p.157
[xv] ibid; p.158
[xvi] Spoto, Donald, *Diana - The Last Year;*; Harmony Books 1997 p. 171
[xvii] Sanction; p.158-9
[xviii] TLC - Mohammed Al-Fayed interview
[xix] Junor, Penny, *Charles - Victim or Villain*; Harper Collins Publishers 1998; p.18
[xx] Sanction; p.167
[xxi] Final Report - Paris Prosecutor's Office; Head of the Prosecution Department at Courts of the First Instance; Examining Magistrates Hervé Stephan and Christine Devidal
[xxii] *TLC* - documentary information
[xxiii] *TLC* - interview with Dr. Martin Skinner.
[xxiv] Anderson; p.191
[xxv] Interview with Mohammed Al Fayed as per his internet site address:www.alfayed.com/indexie4.html, as published to the Internet on October 25, 1998
[xxvi] Spoto; p.172
[xxvii] Sanction; p 251
[xxviii] ibid; p. 6
[xxix] *Newsweek* Magazine; September 8, 1997; p. 33
[xxx] ibid; p. 241
[xxxi] Buchanan, Lyn, *The Seventh Sense*, Paraview Pocket Books, 2003, p. 190
[xxxii] Sanction; p. 17
[xxxiii] ibid; p.17 - 18
[xxxiv] Junor; p. 20
[xxxv] Spoto; p.180
[xxxvi] Junor; p. 22
[xxxvii] *French Final Accident Report* – Conclusionary Statement section
[xxxviii] Lyall, Sarah; New York Times; December 15, 2008

Jack the Ripper

[xxxix] *The Diary of Jack the Ripper* narrative by Shirley Harrison; Hyperion, 1993; Transcript p. 280 hereafter referred to as DJTR

[xl] Ibid; p. 273

[xli] Ibid; p. 140

[xlii] *A History of the Central Synagogue*, Pre 1900, 1900 – 1945, 1945 – 1970; as per various internet sites.

[xliii] *Victoria, An Intimate Biography* by Stanley Weintraub; Truman Talley Books/E.P. Dutton New York 1987; p. 110; hereafter referred to as VIB

[xliv] *Queen Victoria in Her Letters and Journals* a section by Christopher Hibbert; Viking Penguin Inc. 1985; p. 28; hereafter referred to as QV

[xlv] *VIB*; p. 213

[xlvi] *QV*; p. 90

[xlvii] Quoted from the Goteborg tourist information web site, "Centralen"; The History of Goteborg" Web Page as loaded December, 1997.

[xlviii] *Prisoner 1167 - The Madman Who Was Jack the Ripper* by James Tully; Carroll & Graf Publishers, Inc.; 1997; p. 1 hereafter referred to as 1167

[xlix] *Records of the Coroners Inquiry*; South-Eastern Division of Middlesex; Vestry Hall, Cable Street, St. George's-in-the-East hereafter referred to as CI: Sworn testimony of Michael Kidney made Wednesday afternoon October 3, 1888

[l] The dates of the information on Elizabeth Strides' youth and move to England referenced from the base source material in an article by Klas Lithner in a Swedish Journal *Bra on Deckare* No. 60, 1982; p. 14-15 published by Bra Deckare, Sodra vagen, Hoganas, Sweden, and *Elizabeth Stride and Jack the Ripper – The Life and Death of the Reputed Third Victim* by Dave Yost, MacFarland & Company, Inc. Publishers 2008

[li] *CI*; Charles Preston testimony October 3, 1888

[lii] *CI*; Kidney

[liii] *Jack the Ripper - The Uncensored Facts* by Paul Begg; Robson Books; 1988; p. 93, hereafter referred to as *JTRUF*

[liv] *CI*; Kidney

[lv] *VIB*; p. 346

[lvi] *QV*; p. 203

[lvii] *VIB*; p. 349

[lviii] *VIB*; p. 349

[lix] *VIB*; p. 350

[lx] *QV*; p. 206

[lxi] *VIB*; p. 410

[lxii] *VIB*; p. 412

[lxiii] *VIB*; p. 414

[lxiv] *VIB*; p. 424

[lxv] *Man-Made Catastrophes*, by Lee Davis; Facts on File, Inc. 1993; p. 232

[lxvi] *Darkest Hours* by Jay Robert Nash; A Wallace Book published by Pocket Books; 1976; p. 450 hereafter referred to as DH.

[lxvii] *DH*; p.450

[lxviii] *CI*; Preston

[lxix] *CI*; Kidney – co-mingled testimony

[lxx] *CI*; Sven Olsson testimony Friday, October 5, 1888

[lxxi] *CI*; Elizabeth Tanner testimony Thursday, October 4, 1888

[lxxii] *Manchester Guardian, Evening News*; October 8, 1888

[lxxiii] *QV*; p. 252-3

[lxxiv] *VIB*; p. 441

[lxxv] *VIB*; p. 442

[lxxvi] *VIB*; p. 443

[lxxvii] *QV*; p. 262

[lxxviii] *QV*; p. 268

Evidential Details

[lxxix] *QV*; p. 269

[lxxx] *QV*; p. 272

[lxxxi] *1167*; p. 158

[lxxxii] *QV*; p. 291

[lxxxiii] *QV* p. 297

[lxxxiv] *Freud - Dictionary of Psychoanalysis* edited by Nandor Fodor and Frank Gaynor; Fawcett Premier Publications; 1958 p.108 as quoted in *Obsessive Acts and Religious Practices* in Collected Papers, Vol II, hereafter referred to as Freud

[lxxxv] The Report of the Director of the Public Prosecutions', (Public Accounts Committee), Parliamentary Papers (1899) p. 279

[lxxxvi] *CI*; Kidney testimony co-mingled.

[lxxxvii] Thames Magistrates' Court, Court Register, dated April 6, 1887

[lxxxviii] *The Victorian Underground* by Donald Thomas; New York University Press, 1998; p. 298

[lxxxix] *CI*; Preston

[xc] *The Crimes, Detection and Death of Jack the Ripper* by Martin Fido; Barnes & Noble Books, 1993, p. 54. Hereafter referred to as CDDJTR.

[xci] *CI*; Mary Malcolm testimony Wednesday October 3, 1888; testimony co-mingled

[xcii] *The Times*; August 10, 1888

[xciii] *CI*; Catherine Lane testimony Wednesday, October 3, 1888

[xciv] *Manchester Guardian*; October 2, 1888, the statement is attributed to Mrs. Ann Mill, bed maker at the lodging house at #32 Flower and Dean in *JTRA-Z* p. 297

[xcv] *The Portable Karl Marx* Edited by Eugene Kamenka; Penguin Books, 1983

[xcvi] *JTRUF*; p. 187

[xcvii] Charles Letchford - *The London Evening Standard,* 1 October 1888

[xcviii] *Complete History - Jack The Ripper*; p. 227 Hereafter referred to as CHJTR

[xcix] Louis Diemshutz - the *Evening News*; October 1, 1888

[c] Chief Inspector Swanson, Oct. 19, 1888, Home Office records 144/221/ A49301C/ 8a

[ci] *Jack the Ripper A-Z*; complied by Paul Begg, Martin Fido and Keith Skinner; Headline Book Publishing PLC; 1996, p. 42; hereafter referred to as JTRA-Z

[cii] *CHJTR*; p. 166

[ciii] The London Evening Standard, 1 October 1888 - interview with Charles Letchford

[civ] *CI*; William Marshall testimony Friday October 5, 1888

[cv] *CDDJTR*; p. 41

[cvi] Records of the British Home Office 144/AA49301C 8a

[cvii] *CI*; PC William Smith testimony Friday October 5, 1888

[cviii] Israel Schwartz interview - London *Star*, Oct. 1, 1888

[cix] *CI*; Malcolm

[cx] *CI*; Tanner

[cxi] *CI*; Kidney

[cxii] *CHJTR;* p. 209

[cxiii] Interview - *The Times* October 2, 1888

[cxiv] The London Evening Standard, 1 October 1888 - Mrs. Mortimer interview.

[cxv] *CI*; Police Constable Henry Lamb testimony Tuesday October 3, 1888

[cxvi] Deposition; Dr. Blackwell, Oct. 2, 1888 reported in the London *Daily Telegraph; The Daily News* and *The Times* on Oct. 3.

[cxvii] *CI*; Dr. Blackwell testimony Tuesday, October 2, 1888

[cxviii] *JTRUF*; p. 108

[cxix] The London Evening Standard, 1 October 1888 - interview with Charles Letchford

[cxx] Reported in *The Times,* October 2, 1888

[cxxi] The London Evening Standard, 1 October 1888

[cxxii] London Metropolitan Police Special Report #6; November 12, 1888; by witness George Hutchinson

[cxxiii] *QV*; p. 314

[cxxiv] Report written by Sir Melville, Chief Constable Metropolitan Police - February 23, 1894

[cxxv] The Macnaghten Memoranda of February, 1894 – Chief Constable of the CID [Criminal Investigations Division], Scotland Yard as discovered in the possession of his daughter Lady Aberconway and brought forward by Daniel Farson in 1959.

Evidential Details

[cxxvi] *Queen Victoria* by Cecil Woodham-Smith; Dell Publishing Company 1972; p.565 – Appendix 4 as reprinted in total from Sir Phillip Magnus biography of King Edward VII; p. 461

[cxxvii] *The People*; Sunday June 9, 1912 - articles entitled *Scotland Yard and its Secrets* by Hargrave L. Adam

[cxxviii] *The Times*; April 20, 1910

[cxxix] *The Mammouth Book of Jack the Ripper* by Maxim Jakubowski and Nathan Braund; Robinson Publishers, 1999; forgery displayed on p. 97 hereafter referred to as *MB*

[cxxx] *Jack the Ripper: The Final Solution* by Stephen Knight; Academy of Chicago Publishers, 1986 p. 57 hereafter referred to as TFS

[cxxxi] *Inspector Aberline's Press Cuttings Book*; unpublished; complied by Frederick Aberline from 1878 to 1892 including his diary; surrendered to Scotland Yard for editing and final disposition.

[cxxxii] *MB*; p. 468

[cxxxiii] *CI*; Mary Malcolms' testimony, Tuesday Oct. 2, 1888

[cxxxiv] *CI*; Malcolm

[cxxxv] *CI*; Malcolm

[cxxxvi] Report of Chief Inspector Swanson, October 19, 1888

[cxxxvii] *CHJTR*; p.191

[cxxxviii] *JTRA-Z;* p. 431

[cxxxix] *Dictionary of Psychology* by Arthur S. Reber; Penguin Books USA, Inc. 1995, p. 810

[cxl] *Freud*; p. 108 from Collected Papers - Volume I, *'Obsessions and Phobias; their Psychical Mechanisms and their Aetiolog'* and *'Further Remarks on the Defense Psycho-Neuroses'*.

[cxli] *CDDJTR*; p. 55

[cxlii] *Morning Advertiser*, 10 October,1888

[cxliii] *CI*; testimony of Elizabeth Stokes, October. 23, 1888

[cxliv] *CDDJTR*; p. 54

"...He [McMoneagle] served most recently as a Special Project Intelligence Officer for SSPD (Secret Service Protective Division), SSD (Strategic Studies Detachment), and 902d MI (Military Intelligence) Group, as one of the original planners and movers of a unique intelligence project that is revolutionizing the intelligence community. While with SSPD, he used his talents and expertise in the execution of more than 200 missions, addressing over 150 essential elements of information [EEI]. These EEI contained critical intelligence reported at the highest echelons of our military and government, including such national level agencies as the Joint Chiefs of Staff, DIA, NSA, CIA, DEA, and the Secret Service, producing crucial and vital intelligence unavailable from any other source..."

Edwin C. May, Ph.D.
Cognitive Sciences Laboratory, Palo Alto, California
(*The Journal of Parapsychology*. **60**. 3-23. March 1996)

Part III

...as a result of my own previous exposure to this (remote viewing) *community I became persuaded that war can almost always be traced to a failure in intelligence, and that therefore the strongest weapon for peace is good intelligence.*

~ H. E. Puthoff, PhD. ~

Founder and First Director (1972 - 1985)
The U.S. Military Intelligence black ops
Program known as *Operation Star Gate*

Credentials

JOSEPH W. MCMONEAGLE, CW2, US Army, Ret., KCStS
Owner/Executive Director of
Intuitive Intelligence Applications, Inc.

Mr. McMoneagle has over 45 years of professional expertise in research and development, in numerous multi-level technical systems, the paranormal, and the social sciences. Experience includes: experimental protocol design, collection and evaluation of statistical information, prototype design and testing, Automatic Data Processing equipment and technology interface, management, and data systems analysis for mainframe, mini-mainframe, and desktop computer systems supporting information collection and analysis for intelligence purposes.

He is currently owner and Executive Director of Intuitive Intelligence Applications, Inc., which has provided support to multiple research facilities and corporations with a full range of collection applications using Anomalous Cognition (AC) in the production of original and cutting edge information. He is a full time Research Associate with The Laboratories for Fundamental Research, Cognitive Sciences Laboratory, Palo Alto, California, where he has provided consulting support to research and development in remote viewing for 16+ years. As a consultant to SRI-International and Science Applications International Corporation, Inc. from 1984 through 1995, he participated in protocol design, statistical information collection, R&D evaluations, as well as thousands of remote viewing trials in support of both experimental research and active intelligence operations for what is now known as Project STARGATE. He is well versed with developmental theory, methods of application, and current training technologies for remote viewing, as currently applied under strict laboratory controls and oversight.

During his career, Mr. McMoneagle has provided professional intelligence and creative/innovative informational support to the Central Intelligence Agency, Defense Intelligence Agency, National Security Agency, Drug Enforcement Agency, Secret Service, Federal Bureau of Investigation, United States Customs, the National Security Council, most major commands within the Department of Defense, and hundreds of other individuals, companies, and corporations. He is the only one who has successfully demonstrated his ability more than two dozen times, by doing a live remote viewing, double-blind and under controls while on-camera for national networks/labs in four countries.

Mr. McMoneagle has also been responsible for his Military Occupational Specialty at Army Headquarters level, to include control and management of both manned and unmanned sites within the Continental United States, and overseas. He was responsible for all tactical and strategic equipment tasking, including aircraft and vehicles, development of new and current technology, planning, support and maintenance, funding, training, and personnel. He has performed responsibly in international and intra-service negotiations and agreements in support of six national level intelligence agencies, and has acted as a direct consultant to the Commanding General, United States Army Intelligence and Security Command (INSCOM), Washington D.C., as well as the Army Chief of Staff for Intelligence (ACSI), Pentagon.

Other employment has included, Assistant to the Security Officer for a multi-billion dollar overseas intelligence facility, with responsibilities that included physical plant communications, personnel, and technology security; as well as counter-terrorist and counter-intelligence operations. He has served as the Detachment Commander at two remote intelligence collection sites overseas, providing field intelligence collection, analysis and reporting at theater, region, country, and city levels. He has also served on an Air and Sea Rescue team, in Long Range Reconnaissance, as a Quick Reaction Strike Force team leader, and rifleman. He has earned 28 military decorations and numerous awards, to include a Legion of Merit for his AC support to the Nation's Intelligence Community, and he holds the rank of Knight Chevalier in the Order of St. Stanislaus.

Interview Clarification

Question: Generally speaking, how much...information should be given a viewer in operations / applications?

Joseph McMoneagle: None. Zero. What you can do if the target requires a response or a description of an individual, you can say, "Describe the individual at (whatever location)" and the location needs to be hidden (would be a number, for instance). If you were targeting let's say a church, and there was an individual in that church, the church would be coded as say, "location A1". It would then say, "Describe individual at location A1.'"

Under no condition can you give any information that is directly pertinent to the target. There is never any front-loading. The reason for this is because the entire concept of remote viewing is that an individual is forced, has no choice, but to use their psi ability to answer the requirement. Any info that is given in any way, or form, modifies that response in a way that removes / reduces the probability of accuracy.

Human Use

Remote Viewing research sometimes involves input from different sources as in the application of the Army's Human Use Policies developed to protect soldiers from accidental death or impairment.

"In February 1979, the General Counsel, the Army's top lawyer, declared [the Remote Viewing Program called] Grill Flame activities constitute Human Use." The Unit, "...was in the middle of the [authorization] process in March 1979 when the Human Use determination was reversed by the Army Surgeon General's Human Use Subjects Research Review Board. Their decision... trumped the Army General Counsel's ruling...

On November 20, the Surgeon General's board changed its mind and decided that Grill Flame did indeed involve Human Use. It took until February 1, 1982 to get final approval from the Secretary of the Army to continue operations.

New candidates were then issued a warning by a Major General before being accepted into the super-secret 902nd Intelligence Unit.

Among other things, they noted that if he joined the project, he would be exposed to psychic phenomena at a level and with a frequency that most people had never experienced before. As a result, he might change in certain ways. Ultimately, no harm should come to him, but he might have a new perspective on himself, his marriage, the universe. In a sense, he might become a new man, and a new husband."

The candidate and his wife were advised to talk, "...this over before they made the final commitment to go to Fort Meade."

THE 1973 REMOTE VIEWING OF THE PLANET JUPITER'S DISCOVERED RING

(The Planet Jupiter remote viewing) Experiment #46 lay obscure between 1974 and 1979. No continuing attempt was made to feedback other of its categories, and the SRI (Stanford Research Institute) work progressed along more immediately fruitful (confirmational) lines.

(Six years later) The 1979 (Voyager II) scientific discovery and (the July 9, 1979) confirmation of the (Jupiter's) Jovian Ring came as one of the larger shocks - and surprises -- in astronomical history.

A Chinese Encounter

The United States is not the only nation to study and use Remote Viewing. Below is a story allowing enthusiasts and skeptics alike a rare look at life inside the Unit during the middle 1980's.

* * *

"The first time it happened was right after [Major] General Stubblebine had briefed me on the project and said that I would be contacted. The next week I was working mid shift, and one of the afternoons, I lay down for a nap. In that nap, I had a really shallow and lame dream about something I can't remember now. But at one point, right over the top of that dream there was what appeared to be a semi-translucent visual of three people.

One was a very respectable, businesslike slender man in a suit. A second was a very burly, stocky man, also in a suit, and with a very "Texas farmer" face. The third was an ... Oriental girl... (I find it impossible to tell the age of oriental women). She was following along behind the two men and watching.

The men came up to me and talked about something, but I couldn't hear them. The girl was standing behind the two men, listening. The faces were very clear. Clear enough that when the two men actually came to [the INSCOM1 Base in] Augsburg [Germany] to interview me, I recognized them immediately. I could have picked them out of a crowd on the sidewalk. I didn't think anything of the fact that the girl wasn't with them. It would have been odd to have her on a military trip overseas. I thought she was probably some-one in the unit.

Months later, when I got to the unit, she wasn't there. I asked about her and neither the director nor Joe [McMoneagle] (the two men who came to interview me) knew who I was talking about. I figured that it was just an AOL (STRAY CAT)[2] and blew it off.

About a year later, I was doing a practice target. The target was a museum at Arizona State University (I didn't know that - I only had numbers). I was describing things lying in glass topped cases, with the cases up on legs and stands, all arranged around the room for easy access, when I notic-ed that someone at the target site was looking straight at me, as though she

----

1 INSCOM is the abbreviation for the Army's Intelligence and Security Command.
2 Stray Cat is a viewer acronym describing the Subconscious Transfer of Recollections, Anxieties, and Yearnings to Consciously Accessible Thought.

could see me. It startled me and for probably the only time ever, I wasn't startled out of the session, but deeper into it.

I looked back at her, and realized that it was the same girl who had been following the director and Joe in my earlier "dream", back in Augsburg. I looked directly at her, and started to say hello, but then she realized that could see her, too, and she half turned, and disappeared. That threw me out of the session.

Fortunately, [Captain] Paul Smith was my monitor, and ever the curious one, when I told him what had happened, he said, "Let's follow her and see where she went." Through a series of very impromptu movement commands, we finally located her back at the place where she worked ... the Chinese psychic intelligence effort.

She appeared in some of my sessions after that, but rarely. I tried to find her several times, and a few of them succeeded. Apparently, what they defined as "session" and what we defined as "session" weren't the same. Anyway, over time, we struck up somewhat of a stand-offish acquaintance.

About a year after that, I hadn't bumped into her again, so I did a session specifically to find her. She was then in college in a very large city, and evidently out of the government's project altogether. When I found her, she acknowledged my presence, and very strongly desired that we not have further contact. I backed out of the session, and haven't tried again, since. Don't cha love war stories?"[3]

Oct. 1, 1998 e-mail from Leonard Buchanan – Former Operational Database Manager 902nd Military Intelligence Unit - Fort Meade, Maryland and Owner of Problems> Solutions> Innovations, Inc.

You can actually access that person mentally and bring back their most deep-seated thoughts, feelings, emotions, motivations, fears, desires, drives, reservations, and everything else that might be there to drive their actions. It is, perhaps, in this one area where CRV [Controlled Remote Viewing] surpasses any other intelligence tool and finds its highest value.

Operation Star Gate's Data Base Manager Leonard Buchanan – *The Seventh Sense*

---

[3] For more information, see, China's Super Psychics by Paul Dong and Thomas Raffill; Marlowe & Co. New York, 1997

Remote Viewing Data Protocols

Surrounding the military's RV session protocols are the Operational Flow Protocols. The tasking agency was the "Customer" whose identity was strictly withheld to avoid inferences leading to Analytic Overlay. First published here, this process was classified for over two decades.

* * *

"In actual fact, there was pretty much a different work set-up every time we changed directors in the military unit which was pretty often as projects go. As a result, the "ideal plan" was never adhered to. Many times, we had to sort of switch horse in mid-stream. Anyway, here is the "ideal" workflow:

The **CUSTOMER** (Governmental Agency) comes to the unit director with a tasking.
The **UNIT DIRECTOR** meets with the customer and:
1) makes absolutely certain that the customer knows what CRV is and isn't – what it will and won't do.
2) looks the customer's problem over to see that it is the type of work we are best suited for. If not, he suggests a different solution for them.
If so, he then:
3) gets rid of the customer's "test" questions which only take up time and effort and accomplish nothing.
4) gets rid of the unnecessary questions – just fluff questions which the customer would like to have answered.
5) makes certain the questions asked are questions the customer really wants the answers to. There are LOTS of times when the customer will ask, "Who killed the victim", when the information he really wants is, "Where can we find the evidence that will show who killed the victim?"
6) agrees in writing on a set of basic questions which will be answered, once all the fluff and confusion is gotten out of the way.
7) makes certain that the Customer knows that these questions will be answered, and that other information will be provided, if it is found. However, if it isn't found, then the viewers are only responsible for what is being tasked. Follow-on questions will have to be asked later.
8) explains to the Customer the need for accurate feedback.
9) gets a definite commitment from the Customer that such feedback will be given, on each and every viewer's answer(s) to each and every question.
10) sets a commitment date for providing the answers. This must be a realistic date. Every Customer wants answers right now or yesterday, but the unit director needs to impress on the Customer that there are other customers who also have time limits of now or yesterday, and that reality must figure into the planning, like it or not.
11) provides the final list of questions to the Project Officer, along with any background information about the case gained from the customer.

Evidential Details

The **PROJECT OFFICER** studies the background information and tasked questions and:
1) determines the main subject matter for each question.
2) decides the project number and fills out all the preliminary paperwork required for starting a new project.
3) provides the list of subjects to the Data Base Manager. The Data Base Manager looks up each information category in the data base and provides the Project Manager with a separate list of Viewers' names as suggested Viewers for each question.
4) determines which Viewers and Monitors should work on each question.
5) looks at the Viewers' and Monitors' existing schedules and determines the project's time line. He may even do a Pert chart to make scheduling easier.
6) "translates" each question into neutral wording.
7) notifies each Monitor and Viewer of the work schedule change.
8) generates an official tasking sheet to hand to each Monitor.

The **MONITOR** receives the tasking and coordinates from the Project Officer, along with any background information the Project Officer thinks the Monitor should know to help the Viewer better perform a productive session. The Monitor then:
1) makes certain he knows the Viewer's likes and dislikes, quirks, micro-movements, etc. If not, these are either looked up or found out from another Monitor who is more familiar with the Viewer.
2) gets information from the Database Manager about the Viewer's strengths and weaknesses. While this carries the danger of a "self-fulfilling prophecy", the Monitor is hopefully trained enough to use the information for formatting the session, rather than for guiding and leading the Viewer. If the Monitor is not this well trained, this step is passed up.
3) prepares the session workplace.
4) goes through the session with the Viewer.
5) helps the Viewer write the summary, if necessary.
6) after the paperwork is all done, provides both the Viewer's transcript and his (the Monitor's) session notes to the Analyst.

The **ANALYST** receives the paperwork and:
1) familiarizes himself with all the background knowledge.
2) collects the papers from all Viewer/Monitor pairs.
3) looks into his own notes on each and every Viewer to see work profiles (prone to using imagery, prone to using allegories, etc.). The Database Manager can be of help in this step.
4) performs analysis on the session (see the Analyst's Manual).
5) writes up his reports, critiques, summaries, etc. and provides it to the Report Writer.

The **REPORT WRITER** receives all the information from the Analyst and:
1) familiarizes himself with all the available background information.
2) familiarizes himself with all the Analyst's finding, interpretations and comments.
3) writes the final report (see the Report Writer's Manual)

NOTE!!! This includes taking the finalized answer to each Viewer to make certain that what is being reported is what the Viewer actually meant to say.
4) provides the final report to the Project Officer.

The **PROJECT OFFICER** then:
1) receives the finalized answers to each question after the session has been performed, analyzed and prepared for reporting.
2) gives final approval on the final report.
3) passes the final report to the Unit Director for delivery to the Customer.

The **UNIT DIRECTOR** then:
1) contacts the Customer and sets a date and time to go over the report. Information is not given ad hoc over the phone, nor is an "executive summary" provided.
2) meets with the Customer to provide the report.
3) once again makes certain that the Customer understands the CRV process, strengths and limitations.
4) explains what happened, and how each answer was obtained.
5) points out to the Customer that each question has a "dependability rating" beside it which will tell the Customer what each Viewer's track record is on each specific answer to each type of question. He explains how this "dependability rating" can be used by the Customer as an aid to making decisions from the information provided.
6) sets – in writing – a hard and definite "drop dead" date for feedback.
7) if/when feedback comes in, provides it to the Project Officer who handled the case.
8) if feedback doesn't come in, or is received incorrectly, it is returned to the Customer to either, "dun him" for feedback, or to re-explain how feed-back needs to be provided, formatted, etc.

The **PROJECT OFFICER** then:
1) evaluates each Viewer's response to each question against the feedback.
2) provides an evaluation to each Viewer.
3) provides accurate data to the Database Manager for input into the database.
4) completes all summary paperwork for the project.
5) organizes all related paperwork, checks it for completeness, and prepares it for final storage and filing.

The **DATABASE MANAGER**:
1) inputs all received information into the database.
2) "massages" the database to provide information to those who need it. This includes the Training Officer and all Trainers.
3) maintains quality control on the data going in. "Garbage in – garbage out".

The **TRAINING OFFICER**:
1) schedules training times and facilities.
2) keeps evaluation reports on the Trainers.

The **TRAINER**:
1) accompanies new Viewers through the training process, analyzing their needs and   progress every step of the way (see Trainers Manual).

2) makes and keeps records of the Viewer Student's "natural micro-movements". These will be provided to the Monitors along with a Viewer Student's profile of strengths and weakness.

3) advises management of the Viewer Student's progress and advises as to the student's best possible "training track" for providing the most useful and productive Viewer possible.

Needless to say, this is an overview, and not a complete list of responsibilities and obligations. For example, it doesn't cover what goes on in follow-on tasking, etc.

July 23, 1998 e-mail from: Leonard Buchanan– Former Operational Database Manager at the 902nd Military Intelligence Unit - Fort Meade, Maryland and Owner of Problems> Solutions>Innovations, Inc.

Beginnings

This details the basis for the original black ops program funding. For readers interested in the data that justified more Congressional spending, this secretive overview of U.S. Military History is recommended.

CIA-Initiated Remote Viewing
At Stanford Research Institute

H. E. Puthoff, Ph.D.
Institute for Advanced Studies at Austin
4030 Braker Lane W., #300
Austin, Texas 78759-5329

Abstract - In July 1995 the CIA declassified, and approved for release, documents revealing its sponsorship in the 1970s of a program at Stanford Research Institute in Menlo Park, CA, to determine whether such phenomena as remote viewing "might have any utility for intelligence collection" [1]. Thus began disclosure to the public of a two-decade-plus involvement of the intelligence community in the investigation of so-called para-psychological or psi phenomena. Presented here by the program's Founder and first Director (1972 - 1985) is the early history of the program, including discussion of some of the first, now declassified, results that drove early interest.

Introduction

On April 17, 1995, President Clinton issued Executive Order Nr. 1995-4-17, entitled Classified National Security Information. Although in one sense the order simply reaffirmed much of what has been long-standing policy, in another sense there was a clear shift toward more openness. In the opening paragraph, for example, we read: "In recent years, however, dramatic changes have altered, although not eliminated, the national security threats that we confront. These changes provide a greater opportunity to emphasize our commitment to open Government." In the Classification Standards section of the Order this commitment is operationalized by phrases such as "If there is significant doubt about the need to classify information, it shall not be classified." Later in the document, in reference to information that requires continued protection, there even appears the remarkable phrase "In some exceptional cases, however, the need to protect such information may be outweighed by the public interest in disclosure of the information, and in these cases the information should be declassified."

A major fallout of this reframing of attitude toward classification is that there is enormous pressure on those charged with maintaining security to work hard at being responsive to reasonable requests for disclosure. One of the results is that FOIA (Freedom of Information Act) requests that have languished for months to years are suddenly being acted upon.[1]

One outcome of this change in policy is the government's recent admission of its two-decade-plus involvement in funding highly-classified, special access programs in remote viewing (RV) and related psi phenomena, first at Stanford Research Institute (SRI) and then at Science Applications International Corporation (SAIC), both in Menlo Park, CA, supplemented by various in-house government programs. Although almost all of the documentation remains yet classified, in July 1995 270 pages of SRI reports were declassified and released by the CIA, the program's first sponsor [2]. Thus, although through the years columns by Jack Anderson and others had claimed leaks of "psychic spy" programs with such exotic names as Grill Flame, Center Lane, Sunstreak and Star Gate, CIA's release of the SRI reports constitutes the first documented public admission of significant intelligence community involvement in the psi area.

As a consequence of the above, although I had founded the program in early 1972, and had acted as its Director until I left in 1985 to head up the Institute for Advanced Studies at Austin (at which point my colleague Ed May assumed responsibility as Director), it was not until 1995 that I found myself for the first time able to utter in a single sentence the connected acronyms CIA/SRI/RV. In this report I discuss the genesis of the program, report on some of the early, now declassified, results that drove early interest, and outline the general direction the program took as it expanded into a multi-year, multi-site, multi-million-dollar effort to determine whether such phenomena as remote viewing "might have any utility for intelligence collection" [1].

Beginnings

In early 1972, I was involved in laser research at Stanford Research Institute (now called SRI International) in Menlo Park, CA. At that time I was also circulating a proposal to obtain a small grant for some research in quantum biology. In that proposal I had raised the issue whether physical theory as we knew it was capable of describing life processes, and had suggested some measurements involving plants and lower organisms [3]. This proposal was widely circulated, and a copy was sent to Cleve Backster in New York City who was involved in measuring the electrical activity of plants with standard polygraph equipment. New York artist Ingo Swann chanced to see my proposal during a visit to Backster's lab, and wrote me suggesting that if I were interested in investigating the boundary between the physics of the animate and inanimate, I should consider experiments of the parapsychological type. Swann then went on to describe some apparently successful experiments in psychokinesis in which he had participated at Prof. Gertrude Schmeidler's laboratory at the City College of New York. As a result of this correspondence I invited him to visit SRI for a week in June 1972 to demonstrate such effects, frankly, as much out of personal scientific curiosity as anything else.

Prior to Swann's visit I arranged for access to a well-shielded magneto-meter used in a quark-detection experiment in the Physics Department at Stanford University. During our visit to this laboratory, sprung as a surprise to Swann, he appeared to perturb the operation of the magnetometer, located in a vault below the floor of the building and shielded by mu-metal shielding, an aluminum container, copper shielding and a superconducting shield. As if to add insult to injury, he then went on to "remote view" the interior of the apparatus, rendering by drawing a reasonable facsimile of its rather complex (and heretofore unpublished) construction. It was this latter feat that impressed me perhaps even more than the former, as it also eventually did representatives of the intelligence community. I wrote up these observations and circulated it among my scientific colleagues in draft form of what was eventually published as part of a conference proceeding [4].

In a few short weeks a pair of visitors showed up at SRI with the above report in hand. Their credentials showed them to be from the CIA. They knew of my previous background as a Naval Intelligence Officer and then civilian employee at the National Security Agency (NSA) several years earlier, and felt they could discuss their concerns with me openly. There was, they told me, increasing concern in the intelligence community about the level of effort in Soviet parapsychology being funded by the Soviet security services [5]; by Western scientific standards the field was considered nonsense by most working scientists. As a result they had been on the lookout for a research laboratory outside of academia that could handle a quiet, low-profile classified investigation, and SRI appeared to fit the bill. They asked if I could arrange an opportunity for them to carry out some simple experiments with Swann, and, if the tests proved satisfactory, would I consider a pilot program along these lines? I agreed to consider this, and arranged for the requested tests. [2]

The tests were simple, the visitors simply hiding objects in a box and asking Swann to attempt to describe the contents. The results generated in these experiments are perhaps captured most eloquently by the following example. In one test Swann said "I see something small, brown and irregular, sort of like a leaf or something that resembles it, except that it seems very much alive, like it's even moving!" The target chosen by one of the visitors turned out to be a small live moth, which indeed did look like a leaf. Although not all responses were quite so precise, nonetheless the integrated results were sufficiently impressive that in short order an eight-month, $49,909 Biofield Measurements Program was negotiated as a pilot study, a laser colleague Russell Targ who had had a long-time interest and involvement in parapsychology joined the program, and the experimental effort was begun in earnest.

Early Remote Viewing Results

During the eight-month pilot study of remote viewing the effort gradually evolved from the remote viewing of symbols and objects in envelopes and boxes, to the remote viewing of local target sites in the San Francisco Bay area, demarked by outbound experimenters sent to the site under strict protocols devised to prevent artifactual results. Later judging of the results were similarly handled by double-blind protocols designed to foil artifactual matching. Since these results have been presented in detail elsewhere, both in the scientific literature [6-8] and in popular book format [9], I direct the interested reader to these sources. To summarize, over the years the back-and-forth criticism of protocols, refinement of methods, and successful replication of this type of remote viewing in independent laboratories [10-14], has yielded considerable scientific evidence for the reality of the phenomenon. Adding to the strength of these results was the discovery that a growing number of individuals could be found to demon-strate high-quality remote viewing, often to their own surprise, such as the talented Hella Hammid. As a separate issue, however, most convincing to our early program monitors were the results now to be described, generated under their own control.

First, during the collection of data for a formal remote viewing series targeting indoor laboratory apparatus and outdoor locations (a series eventually published in toto in the Proc. IEEE [7]), the CIA contract monitors, ever watchful for possible chicanery, participated as remote viewers them-selves in order to critique the protocols. In this role three separate viewers, designated visitors V1 - V3 in the IEEE paper, contributed seven of the 55 viewings, several of striking quality. Reference to the IEEE paper for a comparison of descriptions/ drawings to pictures of the associated targets, generated by the contract monitors in their own viewings, leaves little doubt as to why the contract monitors came to the conclusion that there was something to remote viewing (see, for example, Figure 1 herein).

As summarized in the Executive Summary of the now-released Final Report [2] of the second year of the program, "The development of this capability at SRI has evolved to the point where visiting CIA personnel with no previous exposure to such concepts have performed well under controlled laboratory conditions (that is, generated target descriptions of sufficiently high quality to permit blind matching of descriptions to targets by independent judges)." What happened next, however, made even these results pale in comparison.

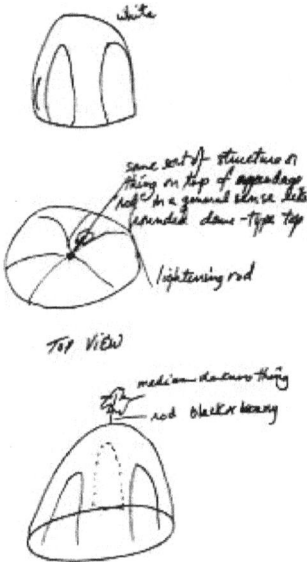

Figure 1 –
Sketch of Target

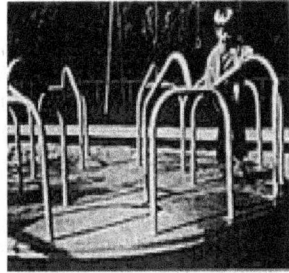

Figure 2 -
Target (merry-go-round)

Coordinate Remote Viewing

To determine whether it was necessary to have a "beacon" individual at the target site, Swann suggested carrying out an experiment to remote view the planet Jupiter before the upcoming NASA Pioneer 10 fly by. In that case, much to his chagrin (and ours) he found a ring around Jupiter, and wondered if perhaps he had remote viewed Saturn by mistake. Our colleagues in astronomy were quite unimpressed as well, until the flyby revealed that an unanticipated ring did in fact exist. [3] Expanding the protocols yet further, Swann proposed a series of experiments in which the target was designated not by sending a "beacon" person to the target site, but rather by the use of geographical coordinates, latitude and longitude in degrees, minutes and seconds. Needless to say, this proposal seemed even more outrageous than "ordinary" remote viewing. The difficulties in taking this proposal seriously, designing protocols to eliminate the possibility of a combination of globe memorization and eidetic or photographic memory, and so forth, are discussed in considerable detail in Reference [9]. Suffice it to say that investigation of this approach, which we designated Scanate (scanning by coordinate), eventually provided us with sufficient evidence to bring it up to the contract monitors and suggest a test under their control. A description of that test and its results, carried out in mid-1973 during the initial pilot study, are best presented by quoting directly from the Executive Summary of the Final Report of the second year's follow-up program [2]. The remote viewers were Ingo Swann and Pat Price, and the entire transcripts are available in the released documents [2].

In order to subject the remote viewing phenomena to a rigorous long distance test under external control, a request for geographical coordinates of a site unknown to subject and experimenters was forwarded to the OSI group responsible for threat analysis in this area. In response, SRI personnel received a set of geographical coordinates (latitude and longitude in degrees, minutes, and seconds) of a facility, hereafter referred to as the West Virginia Site. The experimenters then carried out a remote viewing experiment on a double-blind basis, that is, blind to experimenters as well as subject. The experiment had as its goal the determination of the utility of remote viewing under conditions approximating an operational scenario. Two subjects targeted on the site, a sensitive installation. One subject drew a detailed map of the building and grounds layout, the other provided information about the interior including code words, data subsequently verified by sponsor sources (report available from COTR).[4]

Since details concerning the site's mission in general, [5] and evaluation of the remote viewing test in particular, remain highly classified to this day, all that can be said is that interest in the client community was heightened considerably following this exercise.

Because Price found the above exercise so interesting, as a personal challenge he went on to scan the other side of the globe for a Communist Bloc equivalent and found one located in the Urals, the detailed description of which is also included in Ref. [2]. As with the West Virginia Site, the report for the Urals Site was also verified by personnel in the sponsor organization as being substantially correct.

What makes the West Virginia/Urals Sites viewings so remarkable is that these are not best-ever examples culled out of a longer list; these are literally the first two site-viewings carried out in a simulated operational-type scenario. In fact, for Price these were the very first two remote viewings in our program altogether, and he was invited to participate in yet further experimentation.

Operational Remote Viewing (Semipalatinsk, USSR)

Midway through the second year of the program (July 1974) our CIA sponsor decided to challenge us to provide data on a Soviet site of ongoing operational significance. Pat Price was the remote viewer. A description of the remote viewing, taken from our declassified final report [2], reads as given below. I cite this level of detail to indicate the thought that goes into such an "experiment" to minimize cueing while at the same time being responsive to the requirements of an operational situation. Again, this is not a "best-ever" example from a series of such viewings, but rather the very first operational Soviet target concerning which we were officially tasked. "To determine the utility of remote viewing under operational conditions, a long-distance remote viewing experiment was carried out on a sponsor designated target of current interest, an unidentified research center at Semipalatinsk, USSR.

This experiment, carried out in three phases, was under direct control of the COTR. To begin the experiment, the COTR furnished map coordinates in degrees, minutes and seconds. The only additional information provided was the designation of the target as an R&D test facility. The experimenters then closeted themselves with Subject S1, gave him the map coordinates and indicated the designation of the target as an R&D test facility. A remote-viewing experiment was then carried out. This activity constituted Phase I of the experiment.

Figure 3 shows the subject's graphic effort for building layout; Figure 4 shows the subject's particular attention to a multistory gantry crane he observed at the site. Both results were obtained by the experimenters on a double-blind basis before exposure to any additional COTR-held information, thus eliminating the possibility of cueing. These results were turned over to the client representatives for evaluation. For comparison, an artist's rendering of the site as known to the COTR (but not to the experimenters until later) is shown in Figure 5.

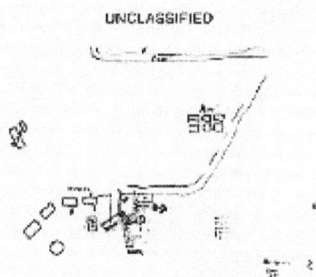

Figure 3 - Subject effort
at building layout

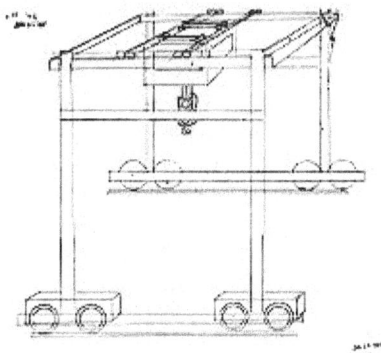

Figure 4 - Subject effort
construction crane

Were the results not promising, the experiment would have stopped at this point. Description of the multistory crane, however, a relatively unusual target item, was taken as indicative of possible target acquisition. Therefore, Phase II was begun, defined by the subject being made "witting" (of the client) by client representatives who introduced themselves to the subject at that point; Phase II also included a second round of experimenttation on the Semipalatinsk site with direct participation of client representatives in which further data were obtained and evaluated. As preparation for this phase, client representatives purposely kept themselves blind to all but general knowledge of the target site to minimize the possibility of cueing. The Phase II effort was focused on the generation of physical data that could be independently verified by other client sources, thus providing a calibration of the process.

The end of Phase II gradually evolved into the first part of Phase III, the generation of unverifiable data concerning the Semipalatinsk site not available to the client, but of operational interest nonetheless. Several hours of tape transcript and a notebook of drawings were generated over a two-week period.

The data describing the Semipalatinsk site were evaluated by the sponsor, and are contained in a separate report. In general, several details concerning the salient technology of the Semipalatinsk site appeared to dovetail with data from other sources, and a number of specific large structural elements were correctly described. The results contained noise along with the signal, but were nonetheless clearly differentiated from the chance results that were generated by control subjects in comparison experiments carried out by the COTR."

For discussion of the ambiance and personal factors involved in carrying out this experiment, along with further detail generated as Price (see Figure 6) "roamed" the facility, including detailed comparison of Price's RV-generated information with later determined "ground-truth reality," see the accompanying article by Russell Targ in the Journal of Scientific Exploration <http:// www. jse.com/>, Vol. 10, No. 1.

Additional experiments having implications for intelligence concerns were carried out, such as the remote viewing of cipher machine type apparatus, and the RV-sorting of sealed envelopes to differentiate those that contained letters with secret writing from those that did not. To discuss these here in detail would take us too far afield, but the interested reader can follow up by referring to the now-declassified project documents [2].

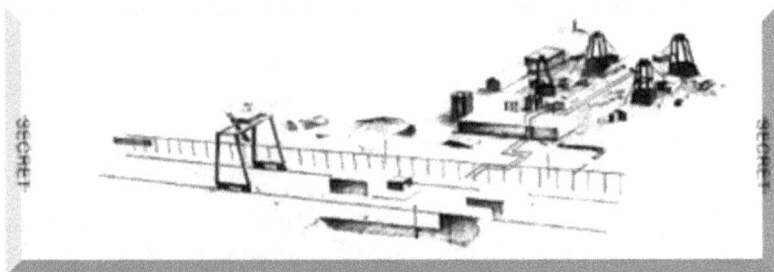

Figure 5 - Actual COTR rendering of Semipalatinsk, USSR target site.

Follow-on Programs

The above discussion brings us up to the end of 1975. As a result of the material being generated by both SRI and CIA remote viewers, interest in the program in government circles, especially within the intelligence community, intensified considerably and led to an ever increasing briefing schedule. This in turn led to an ever-increasing number of clients, contracts and tasking, and therefore expansion of the program to a multi-client base, and eventually to an integrated joint-services program under single-agency (DIA)[6] leadership. To meet the demand for the increased level of effort we first increased our professional staff by inviting Ed May to join the program in 1976, then screened and added to the program a cadre of remote viewers as consultants, and let subcontracts to increase our scope of activity.

As the program expanded, in only a very few cases could the client's identities and program tasking be revealed. Examples include a NASA-funded study negotiated early in the program by Russ Targ to determine whether the internal state of an electronic random-number-generator could be detected by RV processes [16], and a study funded by the Naval Electronics Systems Command to determine whether attempted remote viewing of distant light flashes would induce correlated changes in the viewer's brainwave (EEG) production [17]. For essentially all other projects, during my 14-yr. tenure at SRI, however, the identity of the clients and most of the tasking were classified and remain so today. (The exception was the occasional privately funded study.) We are told, however, that further declassification and release of much of this material is almost certain to occur.

What can be said, then, about further development of the program in the two decades following 1975?[7] In broad terms it can be said that much of the SRI effort was directed not so much toward developing an operational U.S. capability, but rather toward assessing the threat potential of its use against the U.S. by others.

The words 'threat assessment' were often used to describe the program's purpose during its development, especially during the early years. As a result much of the remote-viewing activity was carried out under conditions where ground-truth reality was a priori known or could be determined, such as the description of U.S. facilities and technological developments, the timing of rocket test firings and underground nuclear tests, and the location of individuals and mobile units. And, of course, we were responsive to requests to provide assistance during such events as the loss of an airplane or the taking of hostages, relying on the talents of an increasing cadre of remote-viewer/ consultants, some well-known in the field such as Keith Harary, and many who have not surfaced publicly until recently, such as Joe McMoneagle.

One might ask whether in this program RV-generated information was ever of sufficient significance as to influence decisions at a policy level. This is of course impossible to determine unless policymakers were to come forward with a statement in the affirmative. One example of a possible candidate is a study we performed at SRI during the Carter administration debates concerning proposed deployment of the mobile MX missile system.

In that scenario missiles were to be randomly shuffled from silo to silo in a silo field, in a form of high-tech shell game. In a computer simulation of a twenty-silo field with randomly-assigned (hidden) missile locations, we were able, using RV-generated data, to show rather forcefully that the application of a sophisticated statistical averaging technique (sequential sampling) could in principle permit an adversary to defeat the system. I briefed these results to the appropriate offices at their request, and a written report with the technical details was widely circulated among groups responsible for threat analysis [18], and with some impact. What role, if any, our small contribution played in the mix of factors behind the enormously complex decision to cancel the program will probably never be known, and must of course a priori be considered in all likelihood negligible. Nonetheless, this is a prototypical example of the kind of tasking that by its nature potentially had policy implications.

Figure 6 - Left to right: Dr. Christopher Green, Police Chief Pat Price, and Dr. Hal Puthoff. Picture taken following a successful experiment involving glider to ground RV.

Even though the details of the broad range of experiments, some brilliant successes, many total failures, have not yet been released, we have nonetheless been able to publish summaries of what was learned in these studies about the overall characteristics of remote viewing, as in Table 5 of Reference [8]. Furthermore, over the years we were able to address certain questions of scientific interest in a rigorous way and to publish the results in the open literature. Examples include the apparent lack of attenuation of remote viewing due to seawater shielding (submersible experiments) [8], the amplification of RV performance by use of error-correcting coding techniques [19, 20], and the utility of a technique we call associational remote viewing (ARV) to generate useful predictive information [21].8

As a sociological aside, we note that the overall efficacy of remote viewing in a program like this was not just a scientific issue. For example, when the Semipalatinsk data described earlier was forwarded for analysis, one group declined to get involved because the whole concept was unscientific nonsense, while a second group declined because, even though it might be real, it was possibly demonic; a third group had to be found. And, as in the case of public debate about such phenomena, the program's image was on occasion as likely to be damaged by an over enthusiastic supporter, as by a detractor. Personalities, politics and personal biases were always factors to be dealt with.

Official Statements/Perspectives

With regard to admission by the government of its use of remote viewers under operational conditions, officials have on occasion been relatively forthcoming. President Carter, in a speech to college students in Atlanta in September 1995, is quoted by Reuters as saying that during his administration a plane went down in Zaire, and a meticulous sweep of the African terrain by American spy satellites failed to locate any sign of the wreckage. It was then "without my knowledge" that the head of the CIA (Adm. Stansfield Turner) turned to a woman reputed to have psychic powers. As told by Carter, "she gave some latitude and longitude figures. We focused our satellite cameras on that point and the plane was there." Independently, Turner himself also has admitted the Agency's use of a remote viewer (in this case, Pat Price).[9] And recently, in a segment taped for the British television series Equinox [22], Maj. Gen. Ed Thompson, Assistant Chief of Staff for Intelligence, U.S. Army (1977-1981), volunteered "I had one or more briefings by SRI and was impressed.... The decision I made was to set up a small, in-house, low-cost effort in remote viewing...."
Finally, a recent unclassified report [23] prepared for the CIA by the American Institutes for Research (AIR), concerning a remote viewing effort carried out under a DIA program called Star Gate (discussed in detail elsewhere in this volume), cites the roles of the CIA and DIA in the history of the program, including acknowledgment that a cadre of full-time government employees used remote viewing techniques to respond to tasking from operational military organizations. [10]

As information concerning the various programs spawned by intelligence-community interest is released, and the dialog concerning their scientific and social significance is joined, the results are certain to be hotly debated. Bearing witness to this fact are the companion articles in this volume by Ed May, Director of the SRI and SAIC programs since 1985, and by Jessica Utts and Ray Hyman, consultants on the AIR evaluation cited above. These articles address in part the AIR study. That study, limited in scope to a small fragment of the overall program effort, resulted in a conclusion that although laboratory research showed statistically significant results, use of remote viewing in intelligence gathering was not warranted.

Regardless of one's a priori position, however, an unimpassioned observer cannot help but attest to the following fact. Despite the ambiguities inherent in the type of exploration covered in these programs, the integrated results appear to provide unequivocal evidence of a human capacity to access events remote in space and time, however falteringly, by some cognitive process not yet understood. My years of involvement as a research manager in these programs have left me with the conviction that this fact must be taken into account in any attempt to develop an unbiased picture of the structure of reality.

Footnotes

1 - One example being the release of documents that are the subject of this report - see the memoir by Russell Targ.

2 - Since the reputation of the intelligence services is mixed among members of the general populace, I have on occasion been challenged as to why I would agree to cooperate with the CIA or other elements of the intelligence community in this work. My answer is simply that as a result of my own previous exposure to this community I became persuaded that war can almost always be traced to a failure in intelligence, and that therefore the strongest weapon for peace is good intelligence.

3 - This result was published by us in advance of the ring's discovery [9].

4 - Editor's footnote added here: COTR - Contracting Officer's Technical Representative.

5 - An NSA listening post at the Navy's Sugar Grove facility, according to intelligence-community chronicler Bamford [15]

6 - DIA - Defense Intelligence Agency. The CIA dropped out as a major player in the mid-seventies due to pressure on the Agency (unrelated to the RV Program) from the Church-Pike Congressional Committee.

7 - See also the contribution by Ed May elsewhere in this volume concerning his experiences from 1985 on during his tenure as Director.

8 - For example, one application of this technique yielded not only a published, statistically significant result, but also a return of $26,000 in 30 days in the silver futures market [21].

9 - The direct quote is given in Targ's contribution elsewhere in this volume.

10 - "From 1986 to the first quarter of FY 1995, the DoD para-normal psychology program received more than 200 tasks from operational military organizations requesting that the program staff apply a paranormal psychological technique know (sic) as "remote viewing" (RV) to attain information unavailable from other sources." [23]

References

[1] "CIA Statement on 'Remote Viewing," CIA Public Affairs Office, 6 September 1995.

[2] Harold E. Puthoff and Russell Targ, "Perceptual Augmentation Techniques," SRI Progress Report No. 3 (31 Oct. 1974) and Final Report (1 Dec. 1975) to the CIA, covering the period January 1974 through February 1975, the second year of the program. This effort was funded at the level of $149,555.

[3] H. E. Puthoff, "Toward a Quantum Theory of Life Process," unpubl proposal, Stanford Research Institute (1972).

[4] H. E. Puthoff and R. Targ, "Physics, Entropy and Psycho-kinesis," in Proc. Conf. Quantum Physics and Parapsychology (Geneva, Switzerland); (New York: Parapsychology Foundation, 1975).

[5] Documented in "Paraphysics R&D - Warsaw Pact (U)," DST-1810S-202-78, Defense Intelligence Agency (30 March 1978).

[6] R. Targ and H. E. Puthoff, "Information Transfer under Conditions of Sensory Shielding," Nature 252, 602 (1974).

[7] H. E. Puthoff and R. Targ, "A Perceptual Channel for Information Transfer over Kilometer Distances: Historical Perspective and Recent Research," Proc. IEEE 64, 329 (1976).

[8] H. E. Puthoff, R. Targ and E. C. May, "Experimental Psi Research: Implications for Physics," in The Role of Consciousness in the Physical World", edited by R. G. Jahn (AAAS Selected Symposium 57, Westview Press, Boulder, 1981).

[9] R. Targ and H. E. Puthoff, Mind Reach (Delacorte Press, New York, 1977).

[10] J. P. Bisaha and B. J. Dunne, "Multiple Subject and Long-Distance Precognitive Remote Viewing of Geographical Locations," in Mind at Large, edited by C. T. Tart, H. E. Puthoff and R. Targ (Praeger, New York, 1979), p. 107.

[11] B. J. Dunne and J. P. Bisaha, "Precognitive Remote Viewing in the Chicago Area: a Replication of the Stanford Experiment," J. Parapsychology 43, 17 (1979).

[12] R. G. Jahn, "The Persistent Paradox of Psychic Phenomena: An Engineering Perspective," Proc. IEEE 70, 136 (1982).

[13] R. G. Jahn and B. J. Dunne, "On the Quantum Mechanics of Consciousness with Application to Anomalous Phenomena," Found. Phys. 16, 721 (1986).

[14] R. G. Jahn and B. J. Dunne, Margins of Reality (Harcourt, Brace and Jovanovich, New York, 1987).

[15] J. Bamford, The Puzzle Palace (Penguin Books, New York, 1983) pp. 218-222.

[16] R. Targ, P. Cole and H. E. Puthoff, "Techniques to Enhance Man/ Machine Communication," Stanford Research Institute Final Report on NASA Project NAS7-100 (August 1974).

[17] R. Targ, E. C. May, H. E. Puthoff, D. Galin and R. Ornstein, "Sensing of Remote EM Sources (Physiological Correlates)," SRI Intern'l Final Report on Naval Electronics Systems Command Project N00039-76-C-0077, covering the period November 1975 - to October 1976 (April 1978).

[18] H. E. Puthoff, "Feasibility Study on the Vulnerability of the MPS System to RV Detection Techniques," SRI Internal Report, 15 April 1979; revised 2 May 1979.

[19] H. E. Puthoff, "Calculator-Assisted Psi Amplification," Research in Parapsychology 1984, edited by Rhea White and J. Solfvin (Scarecrow Press, Metuchen, NJ, 1985), p. 48.

[20] H. E. Puthoff, "Calculator-Assisted Psi Amplification II: Use of the Sequential-Sampling Technique as a Variable-Length Majority-Vote Code," Research in Parapsychology 1985, edited by D. Weiner and D. Radin (Scarecrow Press, Metuchen, NJ, 1986), p. 73.

[21] H. E. Puthoff, "ARV (Associational Remote Viewing) Applications," Research in Parapsychology 1984, edited by Rhea White and J. Solfvin (Scarecrow Press, Metuchen, NJ, 1985), p. 121.

[22] "The Real X-Files", Independent Channel 4, England (shown 27 August 1995); to be shown in the U.S. on the Discovery Channel.

[23] M. D. Mumford, A. M. Rose and D. Goslin, "An Evaluation of Remote Viewing: Research and Applications", American Institutes for Research (September 29, 1995).

"Experts" are opposed to the process. Most remain ignorant of - and refuse to learn about - controlled remote viewing. Lifelong subject specialists have books that are suddenly disputed rendering their published conclusions dubious. Others make a living on epochal stories and attempt to stand above being contradicted. Some see everything through religious bias and take exception on the basis the process is paranormal. Others object on the grounds of a potentially besmirched family lineage. And historical revisionists tend to see accurate detail as a hindrance to their design on educational texts. Suffice it to say that it was almost impossible to find someone against this effort - that was not conflicted.

Targeted Reading

Because of its capabilities Remote Viewing disinformation exists in order to discourage further interest. This list was assembled to help people locate books directly from members of the program involved in this most fascinating component of United States Military History.

Books by Members of the U.S. Military Program

McMoneagle, Joseph W.
- *Mind Trek*; Hampton Roads, 1993
- *The Ultimate Time Machine*; Hampton Roads, 1998
- *Remote Viewing Secrets*; Hampton Roads, 2000
- *The Stargate Chronicles*; Hampton Roads, 2002
- *Memoirs of a Psychic Spy*: The Remarkable Life of U. S.
  Government Remote Viewer 001; Hampton Roads, 2006

Buchanan, Leonard
- *The Seventh Sense* – The Secrets of Remote Viewing as Told by a
  "Psychic Spy" for the U.S. Military; Paraview Pocket Books, 2003
- *Remote Viewing Methods* - Remote Viewing and Remote Influencing;
  DVD, 2004

Smith, Paul H.
- *Reading the Enemy's Mind* - Inside Stargate - America's Psychic
  Espionage Program; Tor non-fiction, 2005

Morehouse, David A.
- *Psychic Warrior* – Inside the CIA's Stargate Program: The True Story of a
  Soldiers Espionage and Awakening; St Martin's Press, 1996
- *Nonlethal Weapons: War Without Death*; Praeger Publishers, 1996
- *Remote Viewing*: The Complete User's Manual for Coordinate Remote
  Viewing; Sounds True Publishers, 2011

Puthoff, Harold E. with Russell Targ
- *Mind Reach* - Scientists Look at Psychic Abilities; Delacorte, 1977 & New
  World Library, 2004

Swann, Ingo
- *To Kiss the Earth Goodbye*; Hawthorne, New York, 1975
- *Star Fire*, Dell non-fiction, 1978
- *Natural ESP*: The ESP Core and its Raw Characteristics with Harold E.
  Puthoff; Bantam Books, 1987
- *Everybody's Guide to Natural ESP*: Unlocking the Extrasensory Power of
  Your Mind; Jeremy P. Tharcher Imprint, 1991
- *Your Nostradamus Factor*, Fireside Press, 1993
- *Remote Viewing & ESP From The Inside Out*; DVD

Targ, Russell
- *Mind Race:* Understanding and Using Psychic Abilities, with Keith
  Harary; Ballantine Books, 1984

- *Miracles of Mind:* Exploring Nonlocal Consciousness and Spiritual Healing; New World Library, 1999
- *Limitless Mind:* A Guide to Remote Viewing and Transformation of Consciousness; New World Library, 2004
- *Do you See What I See*?; ESP and the C.I.A. and the Meaning of Life; Hampton Roads, 2010
- *The Reality of ESP*: A Physicists Proof of Psychic Abilities; Quest Books, 2012

Atwater, F. Holmes
- *Captain of My Ship, Master of My Soul*: Living with Guidance; Hampton Roads Publishing, 2001

Other Sources

Monroe, Robert
- *Journeys Out of the Body*; Three Rivers Press, 1992
- *Ultimate Journey*; Three Rivers Press, 1996

Radin, Dean I.
- *The Conscious Universe*: The Scientific Truth of Psychic Phenomena; Harper Edge, 1997

- *Entangled Minds:* Extrasensory Experiences in a Quantum Reality, Paraview Pocket Books, 2006

Moreno, Jonathon D. - *Mind Wars*: Brain Science and the Military in the 21st Century; Bellevue Literary Press, 2012

Schnabel, Jim – *Remote Viewers*: The Secret History of America's Psychic Spies; Dell–non-fiction, 1997

McRae, Ronald – *Mind Wars:* The true story of Government Research into the Military Potential of Psychic Weapons; St Martin's Press, 1984

Additional Taskings

Lae City Airport, New Guinea - July, 1937 – Get into the cockpit for the last flight of the vanished pilot **Amelia Earhart**. Learn of the plane's unknown final flight trajectory, cockpit circumstances and **final thoughts in her last minute of life**. Entered into four libraries within six months, including Purdue University's Earhart Special Collection Library, the book includes a "how to find the **debris field" location map** with yardages and points of reference including a flight scenario that has never been put forward. With the continuous failures of the TIGHAR Group, insiders have subsequently blogged that the Southeast end scenario is the one worth investigating.

Evidential Details

Ötzal Alps Mountains - Italian-Austrian border ~ 3,300 BC – Follow the trail of Europe's archeological "show of the century". Learn the whereabouts of **Ötzi the Iceman**'s unknown home camp and why and how he died alone in the mountains which some still regard as a Neolithic crime scene. This book includes remote viewing maps, pre-death tool drawings, including an undiscovered tool, his cabin, and **the world's only real time portrait** considered significant enough that the Museum in Bolzano, Italy obtained its copywrite release for Ötzi's 20th Anniversary exhibit. Interwoven with scientific quotation, this account also includes specifics of **his tribal life** in what we first identified as the Langtaufers Valley. The book provides Ötzi's previously unknown eight day course through the mountains using modern Alpine trail numbers. Learn the cause for his **violent death** which is the only solution that explains the other theories.

RMS Titanic - North Atlantic – Midnight April, 1912 – In the first book to appear since the revelations of the 2nd Officer's granddaughter, review the Evidential Details substantiating the **amazing crow's nest developments** as Titanic bore down on the ice. Then, move to a resolution regarding **Captain E. J. Smith's final actions** in his previously unknown non-drowning death. The book includes obscure artifact drawings whose existence was only confirmed through ocean floor salvage after these sessions. Once the last lifeboat was away, those left behind knew death was imminent. Read History's only narrative of the last 20 minutes as the ship prepared to take over 1500 terrified passengers into the frigid black ocean at 2:18 am.

U.S. Civil War, The Maryland Campaign - September, 1862 – Considered an unsolvable whodunit, this little known, but most significant mystery in America's Civil War resolves who lost Confederate General Robert E. Lee's **top secret Special Order 191**. The result was the battles of South Mountain and Harper's Ferry, leading directly to the bloodiest day in American History at **Antietam Creek**. The upshot was the timing of the Emancipation Proclamation that legalized the election of Barak Obama. With information from the National Park Service, the book provides aerial campground maps and reveals the previously unknown who, why, when, where and how these orders found their way into the Union General's hands. This book also provides the world's first clinical determination on Union Commander George McClellan's psychological problems.

Last Stand Hill - Little Big Horn River - Montana - June, 1876 – This is History's only documentation of **General George Armstrong Custer**'s last stand from the viewpoints of the victors and the vanquished. Read about **Chief Sitting Bull**'s as well as Custer's battle thoughts. Learn of his true cause of Custer's death and the amazing reasons his body is likely not in his tomb at West Point. You get new, remote viewing generated, battle maps with a drawing of Custer's last fighting stance, a near death facial close-up drawing and, since he was never photographed, **the world's only full page portrait of Indian War Chief Crazy Horse**.

Execution Square - Rouen, France - May, 1431 – Go to the stake in the market square for the ghastly burning of the military heroine lost in the mists of time - **Joan of Arc**. Highlighted are her military successes, capture, and some trial excerpts. These sessions provide an amazingly detailed architectural description of Rouen's medieval square exactly as Joan saw it. Learn of the prosecutor's motivations and the fear of the spectators and the British soldiers. McMoneagle's renowned artwork documents the scene when she was chained to the burning scaffold and includes **History's only portrait of this previously faceless Saint.**

The Unprecedented Series of
Non-fiction Evidential Details Mysteries Solved.

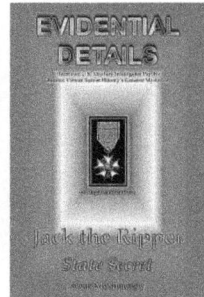

My library
Was dukedom large enough.

Shakespeare in *The Tempest*

www.ingramcontent.com/pod-product-compliance
Lightning Source LLC
Chambersburg PA
CBHW022025090426
42739CB00006BA/293